Always Believe In Yourself

Steven B Osborne

Copyright © 2013 Steven B Osborne

All rights reserved.

ISBN-13: 978-1490925400
ISBN-10: 1490925406

NOTE FROM AUTHOR

This is not a story about Rags to Riches but a true life account of how you can make it if you
ALWAYS BELIEVE IN YOURSELF
From a working class family and a not so happy child hood I was evicted from the family home at the age of 14 years and slept on the streets of London. I worked in a Wimpy Bar and worked on a fruit / veg stall before joining the British Army. This book is not like other Army books that have been written like when I was in the SAS and I took on 100 men and won. No this book is all about the fun the laughs and the cock ups I made during my 22 years 268 days service. I have tried to show you by writing this book a lighter side of life in the Army which is not always written about. If there are young people out there that are thinking of joining the Military perhaps after reading this your decision will be made a lot easier.
Steven B Osborne

ABBREVIATIONS

AAI	ANGLE OF APPROACH INDICATOR
ASAP	AS SOON AS POSSIBLE
BATUS	BRITISH ARMY TRAINING UNIT SUFFIELD
BRATTIES	GERMAN SAUSAGE
BV 206	BANDVAN 206 SWEDISH TRACKED VEHICLE IN THE ARTIC
CO	COMMANDING OFFICER
CPL	CORPORAL
EOD	EXPLOSIVE ORDINANCE DISPOSAL
EPC (A)	EDUCATION PROMOTION COURSE ADVANCE
HH	HELICOPTER HANDLER
HGV	HEAVY GOODS VEHICLE
HQ	HEAD QUARTERS
LT	LIEUTENANT
2 I/C	SECOND IN COMMAND
MOD	MINISTRY OF DEFENCE
NBC	NUCLEAR BIOLOGICAL CHEMICAL
NCO	NON COMMISSIONED OFFICER
NAAFI	NAVY ARMY AIR FORCE INSTITUTE
NIG	NEW IN GERMANY
NI	NORTHERN IRELAND
OC	OFFICER COMMANDING
OPS	OPERATIONS WAGGON/ROOM
PMC	PRESIDENT MESS COMMITTEE
POD	PETROL OR DIESEL
QM	QUARTER MASTER STORES
RSM	REGIMENTAL SERGEANT MAJOR
R-R	REST AND RECUPERATION
SSGT/SGT	STAFF SERGEANT/SARGEANT
SMQC	SENIOR MILITARY QUALIFICATION COURSE
SNCO	SENIOR NONCOMMISSION OFFICER
SQN	SQUADRON
SSM	SQUADRON SERGEANT MAJOR
SLR	SELF LOADING RIFLE
TCWO	TRANSPORT CONTROL WARRANT OFFICER
TRG	TRAINING
TTF	TRUCK TANKER FEUL
UBRE	UNIT BULK REFUELLING EQUIPMENT

Always Believe In Yourself

The room was small but large enough for a desk to be sat at an angle at the back of the room. Behind the desk was a large man aged around 35 who I am certain would have been a lot slimmer in his youth. but who was I to comment on others, when I was standing there 6ft tall with a size 12 neck, a 36 inch chest, and arms as big as straws, a 28 inch waist, and a few teenage spots thrown in for good measure. There was a three drawer filling cabinet in the corner of the room on which sat a kettle and a couple of cups. A small window let some light into the room, and in the rays of light you could see the particles of dust swirling around in the air. I was told to sit down by the large gentlemen behind the desk, and there I was sat on a single wooden chair that had seen better days, staring at two different objects in front of me. The first one being the oversized human about 3ft from me, he was wearing a shirt and tie and a heavily ironed jumper. The knot of his tie was poking out over the top of his jumper as if it was trying to escape from his neck. I could only see the bottom of his trousers which sat above his boots, which on first glance looked like they were made of glass .The second object was two pieces of A4 paper held together by a single staple, with the top copy folded back revealing the 2nd sheet. This only had a couple of lines typed onto it, but half way down the page there it was staring at me a two inch long solid black line with the word signature next to it. I sat and looked at it for what seemed like an hour, when I was brought out of my thoughts by the words "here's a pen sign" and like a robot I signed, and that was it I had just joined the British Army. I was 17 years and 4 months old when I put pen to paper, and I had just committed myself to serve 22 years with an option of 9. this meant that I had to serve at least 9 years before I could get out of the army, what was I thinking ?.

I WOULD LIKE TO SAY THANK YOU
FOR PURCHASING THIS BOOK.
ONE POUND FROM EVERY BOOK
SALE WILL BE DONATED TO
THE ROYAL BRITISH LEGION

CHAPTER ONE

My early life was like most children's of working class parents in the sixties, not a lot of money to go around but there was always food on the table, no matter who's house you were in, that's something I will always remember as a kid. If my parents were working and they were not in the house when I came home from school, I would go to my mate's house where it was never a problem for them to feed me.

I have some good, bad, and funny memories of my early childhood, like the time I got my little sister to light some matches and put them on top of some screwed up paper, that I had placed on the kitchen floor. Well up it went, the lino started to melt on the floor, and the flames had started to burn the wooden sink cabinet, plus there was loads of smoke puffing up everywhere. This is great I thought a six year old has built his own bonfire, roll on firework night. The problem was it was a Sunday morning and both parents were still in the sack sleeping, and the 5th of November was months away.

The bedroom door flies open and this demented man (my father) comes screaming and yelling out of the bedroom, waving his arms and legs about and going around in circles. I remember immediately hiding under the table in the fetal position, and watching my father's attempt to put out the fire, which my sister had started. Oh yes that's what I told my mother and father when the fire was out. It wasn't me, but it didn't work, I got a beating and a half and my sister got picked up and loved. That event set the playing field for the next eight years of my life; I had become the Black Sheep of the family.

School was fun and so it should be, you go to school to learn and get an education, so you have a better chance in life, that's what my father drummed into me daily. The school report would arrive by post and my heart would sink, I would be in the bedroom waiting for the call which wouldn't be long in coming. "Steven get down here" what's this? he would say, do you not want to get a good job when you leave school, do you not want to be successful in life, or do you want to be a road sweeper, or a drop out."

Each report from various teachers would all read the same (Steven needs to concentrate more on his work and stop distracting others with his foolish behavior). I was good at school I could understand and learn much quicker than some of the others, but my attention span was about 10 seconds, then I would get bored and start mucking about with the others, who I might add were bored just like me. When I failed my eleven plus exam that was another nail in my coffin. My parents had plans for me to go to a grammar school, and were deflated to say the least, when I had failed the test. The truth was I did not want to go to a posh grammar school, I wanted to be with my mates who I had grown up with and if they were not going to a grammar school nor was I.

So there we were living in Kingston upon Thames the Royal Borough I might add, and I was off to Rivermead boy's school with all my mates. I tried to settle down and done well in my 1st year, my report was good and my parents were on my side for once.

But like everything else that was all to change and I blame it all on my musical ambitions. As a thirteen or fourteen year old in the early 70s, you were in awe of the rock groups around at that time, to many to mention. I decided that I was going to be a rock star, so I started to go to music lessons. The music teacher was a honey I was in love with her, so were all the other kids and I bet some of the teachers were as well. We have all been there as young boys, fantasizing that one day you will be with this person who is twice as old as you.

Lessons continued and in a few weeks' time there was going to be a school concert, where all budding musicians would compete against each other. The evening of the event finally arrived and the school assembly room was packed with parents. I think I was about seventh to come on, so not to long for my parents to wait and see a budding musician in the making. A couple of kids before me played the Trumpet and Sax, some boy played a piece of some piano concerto he was very good, and then it was my turn to impress the public.

Silence filled the hall and I walked on to a generous applause. I took up my place in front of the microphone, put my hand in my pocket and pulled out my mouth organ (harmonica). I played one verse of MICHEAL ROW THE BOAT ASHORE and then said "thank you" and walked of the stage, and that was my act. After my performance I made my way to see my parents, only to find, that the seats they had been sat in were now empty. They had both got up and had left the school and gone home.

So there I was without a lift home, it was raining, my parents were not impressed and I was getting wet. On walking in the door I was met with these words from my father. "You are an embarrassment to the family, and an embarrassment to yourself you're worthless". Those words sat in my head for years, and I realised I was not part and never had been part of the family.

So I went back to my normal ways, having fun misbehaving and getting introduced to the cane. I can still remember the words being said to me by the house master "bend over young Osborne this will hurt me more then it will hurt you"(how). You hear the cane sweeping down through the air and in a split second it makes contact with your arse, wow that hurts and the good thing is you have 5 more to come. After the canning you rush down to the toilets and say to your mates "is it bleeding" oh yes 6 lines seeping blood, that's it I'm going to sue them, I'm going to the police that's what I'm going to do yeah yeah ,yeah, give it a dab with loo roll and get on with life

I got myself into the local newspaper which I was quite proud of, but again my parents were not. I was fourteen and the 5th years had somehow gone on strike, they were refusing to go back into the class rooms. This was great I thought so I went and joined them sitting there singing "we shall not be moved." I never noticed the local press and there I was front page arms wide apart, cigarette in hand singing at the top of my voice. By now both my parents had given up on me. I even had my own key to come and go as I liked., But I still got the beatings and the constant verbal abuse, (you're a failure and an embarrassment to the family).

So I started to spend more time at my granddads house, he was a great man who thought the sun shone out of my backside and I loved being there. I was a completely different kid when I was with him. He would talk to me about the army and what he had done, plus all the fun he had while serving, and how it had changed his life. He loved telling me his stories and I just loved listening to them. My summer holidays would be spent with my granddad all 5 weeks of them, where he would walk me around all the museums in London. The War Museum was a must, nothing ever changed inside, but we had to visit it every time I stayed with him.

I was nearly 15 years of age when I got expelled from school, I had thrown a golf ball across the playground and it bounced and hit a teacher who was on playground duty. It was not meant to hit the teacher, but all my so called mates all seemed to point their fingers at me, so that was it I was expelled. I never said anything to my parents when I got home that day; my plan was to intercept the letter and throw it away the next morning. I was up early and was hovering around the front door waiting for the postman, but had to go upstairs for something, and it was then that I heard the noise of the letter box. I waited and waited and then an explosion of noise filled the house.

I was told to get out of the house and do not return, I was an embarrassment, I was worthless, in fact I was just a waster. I had heard it all before so I went upstairs, grabbed a holdall, took my toothbrush, T-shirt and a pair of jeans and went back down stairs. I then grabbed my jacket and took about five pounds in cash that was on the table, I opened the front door and left the house and I never went back.

CHAPTER TWO

I was cold, damp, and chilled to the bone, I was unwashed, my clothes were dirty, I was very tired, and I was feeling all alone. Welcome to the real world, I was spending my third night in an old London telephone box. During the day I would walk around looking for something to do. I was lonely I had no mates around me, it was just me and my thoughts, which were, wow is this it, is this the real world? Each evening I would go to a Chinese take away and would buy a bag of chips and a cup of tea. The cost of this great meal would be one pound, and as I only had about 5 pounds on me, I knew my meals were numbered. At night I would go and sit in the phone box and try to sleep until morning, then I would go and do what I had done on the previous days, and that was to look for a job.

In those days the telephone boxes had the telephone directories fitted inside the phone box. I ripped one of the directories of the shelf, and used it to sit on and keep my bum off of the ground. I got some old newspapers and used these to plug up the small gaps between the phone box and the ground. There was no way was I going to go home (not that I was wanted anyway) and I was out to prove to everyone, including myself that I could make it on my own.

I could not go to my granddads because he had passed away a few weeks before I got expelled from school, but I always remembered this one bit of advice he gave me. Stand on your own two feet son, the only person who can help you is you, and always be confident in everything you do.

After five nights in my little home I was walking around when I noticed a piece of paper stuck on a Wimpey Bar window advertising kitchen staff wanted. so in I went. I spoke to a man called Fernando who was later to be a great help, and after I had told him everything about me he offered me the job. He knew of a place where I could stay albeit with other young homeless people, but who cares, I was out of the phone box, and in a room with two other lads who were older than me.

Start work 9am finish at 1am, my breakfast, lunch, and evening meal were all free, plus I got a wage of about ninety pounds for a six day week.

I had made it; I had got my first job at fourteen years of age. Fernando gave me a little advance on my 1st wage, this was so I could buy a couple of things like soap, toothpaste, just the basics and away I went, head down full steam ahead feeling confident and into the kitchen.

A little serving hatch was my only view to what was happening out on the floor, but the plates, cups, ice cream sundae dishes just kept arriving at the hatch. Scrape the food into the bin, stack all the plates etc. onto a dish washer draw, put the draw into the washer turn on, then dry everything by hand it was great. I had a potato peeler behind me which was on constantly peeling away, and four metal dustbins full of chips sat in water waiting to go out to the fryer. Keeping the restaurant floor swept and moped was also part of the job, not a problem give me more work I was not going to fail.

Some of the thing that would come back on the plates was odd to say the least apart from food I had...... Fag ends put out on the plates, sun glasses, a wallet, and a top set of teeth. On seeing these I cleaned them and went out onto the floor, looking for a customer with the top of their mouth collapsed. And there she was looking everywhere for her teeth, on handing over her top set she said "thanks sonny" got up and walked out.

I could not take my wages home with me as it would have gone missing. I was too young to open a bank account, I had moved away from the people who I could have trusted, and so Fernando became my bank. He kept an account of my money, so did I, and I knew it was safe. After about nine months I was no longer in the kitchen, I was now working the floor as the waiter. I would also help out the chef here and there, and fry a few burgers when I got the chance.

It was the chef's holiday and Fernando asked if I would do the cooking for a couple of weeks, not a problem said I, and jumped straight in with bags of confidence. It was then that I realized what I wanted in life, and that was TO BE IN CHARGE. I was in charge of everything, no matter how quick the waiters were with their orders; I had the food ready for them. If only my mother and father could see me now, they would have to have eaten their spiteful comments, calling me a waster, lowlife, and an embarrassment, where were they now?, nowhere to be seen. In fact my parents had never once informed the police that I was even missing, or asked about my whereabouts.

I then made a big mistake, I was letting the odd burger and chips go out on the take away side, and would not charge for it. These were people who I was living with and needed food, they never had a job, so I thought well what's a burger, well in fact it cost me my job. Fernando asked me if I was letting the odd burger go out the side window for free, I had to own up and tried all the waffle and excuses I could think of, but it was out of his hands and I was sacked.

CHAPTER THREE

That's another box of bananas packed because that was what I was doing now. weighing each hand of bananas, placing the price sticker on them, and then putting them in a box. I had left the accommodation that I was in while I had worked for Wimpey's, and had collected nearly 8 months of wages from Fernando. I had moved on and had found a room to rent and got this job. I had to be at work for 0600hrs and I would finish at 1600hrs Monday to Friday. You would qualify for a bonus, if you turned up on time, and completed a whole weeks work. They would give you a whopping 25lb of bananas to take home.
Now what can you do with that amount of bananas, a lot of the workers never took them home. So they just got packed in the boxes with all the others. Surely I could do something with all these free bananas, and then it hit me why don't I sell them. To set up a stall and try to get a pitch would be impossible, all the pitches would have been sown up in the markets, and there would be a waiting list that's for sure.
So I went to the largest fruit and veg stall holder, and asked him if I could work with him on a Saturday. I gave him a good deal and he took it, and now I was working two jobs. I went and spoke to a few of the packing staff, who never took their bonus, and asked them if they would take it, and then give me, their 25lb of bananas on the Friday. I was pleasantly surprised by the amount of people who said yes. There I was, 4 o'clock on a Friday afternoon, with about 300lb of bananas waiting for Dave the stall holder to turn up with his van. When he turned up his eyes nearly fell out of his head, his first words were "what the fuck are we going to do with this lot", give them away I answered. Are you mad Steve he replied, as he was still trying to come to terms with the amount of bananas facing him. So I explained my thinking to him, he was sceptic, and not convinced, but he was willing to give it a try?
Early Saturday morning and I was at the stall before Dave, I started pulling back the sheets and putting the signs up, basically getting things ready for the day. I was full of energy because I wanted to put my plan into force. Dave appeared with his van and we started to unload the stock, he was still not 100% convinced but he had not paid for the bananas, so what was the problem, anyway I was confident and that was all that mattered. We were open and there I was stood behind mountains of veg, loads of fruit, a set of scales in front of me with lots of little weights, which were so old, it was hard to see what the weight of each one was, but who cared I was there and

in my element.

Time to put my idea into action and knowing Dave was at the other end of the stall and was watching me I went for it. REMEMBER WE ARE IN LONDON

Hello sweetheart what would you like darling, arf a pond of mush no probes darling, couple of pand of tatters, there you go, a small collie, and a few other bits and bobs. By the time she had finished ordering there was a few others waiting to be served. As I gave the women her fruit and veg I said "do you like nanas love?, yer I do son was her reply, so I gave her a small hand of narnies and said "there you go sweetheart, fanks for getting your fruit and veg here, and don't tell the guvnor or he will sack me, and I threw in a laugh.

The old dear was made up and you just knew she had to tell others, but the people who were waiting had seen what I had done and I remember some old boy saying "I like bananas son" this was before he even ordered anything. Within fifteen to twenty minutes the stall was mobbed. Dave was working hard trying to restock the front of the stall, because I was moving a lot of fruit and veg, and the queue was not getting any smaller. It was a fantastic day, and it had flown by, and most of Dave's fruit and veg had been sold, and we had got rid of all the bananas. Dave was very happy and so was I, my idea had worked and Dave gave me a good days pay. I asked him if I was ok for next week, not a problem Steve I will pick you and the stock up on Friday. See you then and I was off, my mind was doing overtime.

Not only had my idea worked, I had also shown a seasoned fruit and veg stall holder, a different way to sell his stock, plus I had got a few extra quid in my pocket. So I went back to my room got showered and went out. I got a burger and chips and then went off to the pub for a few pints of light & bitter. It was not long before I felt a bit drunk, so I went back to my room and lay down, and that's when the room started spinning.

Packing and selling bananas was good fun but I wanted another challenge, I was cock sure of myself and could not see myself doing this for years to come. Not that there is a problem in being a stall holder, we all need them but it was not for me. So I told Dave that I was chucking in the job at the packing plant, and was going to be a carpet salesman for this large well known furniture and carpet store, which was next to the market. He offered me extra money, full time work, but my mind was made up, and who knows I might sell Dave a carpet in the near future, never a true word has been spoken.

I started off in the warehouse first getting the orders ready for the next day delivery, and moving furniture around on the shop floor. You know what I mean, table and chairs here settee over there, that light sits on that table and so on. I was not very good at matching colours, so on a regular basis I would have someone follow me around changing my layouts, so the colours would match, but to me it looked good.

But I wanted to sell carpets, why I haven't a clue, maybe it was the thought of interacting with the public again, like I had been doing when I worked on the stall, and to be honest I did miss that. I was told the boss wants a word, he told me that the other staff had had enough of constantly altering my layouts, so everything would match, (colour coding) and was to start in the carpet department on Monday.

That weekend I read over and over again, what carpet is best for what room, what underlay is best for what carpet, is it hard wearing so on so on. I brought my first suit that weekend and yes me and the colour coding failed again. When I turned up for work, the look on the faces of all the staff was quite intimidating, mouths open, making ugh! noises. What's wrong with these people, I looked smart and was ready to sell carpets. I was wearing my new light grey checked suit, with red piped lines bordering the outline of the squares, a new pair of brown slip on tassels, (fashion at the time) a dark brown shirt to go with the shoes, and a bright Yellow tie, which someone had to tie for me as I had no idea how to tie a tie.

I got the hang of selling carpets pretty quickly, plus I was not afraid to talk to customers, it seemed to come natural to me, and soon I was making good commission. A couple of times I would even out do the other sales staff. I now wanted to find out how to fit the carpets that I was selling to the public. I was allowed to go out one day a week to get some experience and work with the fitting crew. I kept in touch with Dave and we got around to talking carpets, he was interested in getting a new carpet through the whole house so I was the man to help him out, and not even 17 years old yet.

One evening I was in the warehouse with one of the fitters, and we were in the process of loading a 72ft Axminster carpet onto one of the company's vehicles, when I was asked what we were doing, it was the police (shit). I explained I worked in the warehouse, I have the keys and we are just loading up the vehicle now as we have a busy day ahead of us. He seemed to buy the excuse, but when I turned up for work the next day, I was summoned to the manager's office, and sacked there and then. I felt sick and deflated, I was angry with myself for doing a bloody stupid thing and losing a chance to better myself, and for letting down those who trusted in me.

Dave asked if I wanted a job but I declined, but we did have a laugh when we thought of how it must have looked to the policeman, seeing two guys trying to carry out a huge rolled up 72ft long carpet at midnight, what a jerk, but you live and learn, and Dave never carpeted his house, well not for free anyway.

I worked in a bottling factory, where thousands of bottles would get filled with wine on a daily basis. I lasted a couple of weeks and then I had to leave, the fumes were unreal and you were permanently half cut. Plus you got 6 bottles of wine as a bonus if you attended all week, my brain was turning into a vat.

The programme HMS Arc Royal was on the television and I loved it, the thought of being part of a team and doing something worthwhile, visiting exciting places, and getting paid to see the world. So that was it, I would join the Royal Navy, and so of I went to the careers office and sat the test. I was sat outside in the waiting room looking at all the posters, and dreaming of what part of the Navy I was going to go into, when I got called into the office. I was informed that I had passed the written entrance exam; Wow! I had actually passed a written exam for the first time in my life. Who needed to pass their eleven plus, not me I was in the navy, or so I thought.

I was told that I had scored enough to go for the training of an Artificer Apprentice; sounded good never had a clue what he was on about, but went along with it, ok I said sounds great. We just need to see your school reports if that's possible, my world collapsed big time, all my dreams went up in flames in one split second. How can I get out of this one Steve come on think, but it was no good I had to come clean, because they would have found out later on. They said they were sorry but we think you would be better off and suited for the Army. Even though I had always played soldiers when I was a kid, I did not want to join the Army; I wanted to join the Navy. Rod Stewart was in the charts with Sailing and that was what I wanted to do, sail and be in the Navy.

I then tried the fire service but during the medical I was not impressed with a complete stranger feeling my balls and I told him so in no uncertain terms, plus I could not expand my chest 2in which is a requirement you have to achieve, so that went out the window.

I moved down to the Aldershot area home of the British Army, why I have no idea, but I got a job working for a building supplier, which was ok nothing outstanding but it was work. Then one day the foreman said he needed a hand in getting some stores in town so off we went. He parked up outside this shop and while he was in there ordering what he needed, I saw the sign JOIN THE BRITISH ARMY. So I walked away from the van and into the recruiting office, wearing a pair of ripped jeans that were covered in dust, a baggy T shirt, a pair of Doctor Martin boots, and a Harrington jacket. Hello Sir I want to join the Army and that was it, I took the test there and then which I passed, then I swore the allegiance to the Queen, and signed up for 22 years with an option of nine. I still snigger to myself when I think of what the foreman must have thought when he came out of the shop and I was not there, his face must have been a picture.

CHAPTER FOUR

What was all that noise, and who was this man coming towards me shouting and waving his arms about like a demented bull, had he escaped from the local asylum, or was he just having a fit in front of me. Neither, he was in fact a soldier of some rank, and was explaining to me in military language that I was not allowed to smoke, and too put my cigarette out immediately. Instead of saying politely you cannot smoke here, and would you mind putting the cigarette out please, this man had to have this moment of madness, where he was shouting so much he was actually spitting on me. I stood there looking at him which wasn't hard, as he was only about 6 inches from my face and was thinking is this guy for real.

So I dropped the cigarette onto the floor, but this only sent him into another fury of half spoken words, which were unrecognizable to humans, but I quickly worked out that I had to pick up the cigarette butt and fast. Anything to stop this guy from having a heart attack. After what seemed like an eternity he spoke in words that I could understand. There was no smoking except in designated areas, and these are clearly marked, and there's especially no smoking outside the Quartermasters Store.

As he turned away I was left thinking, I can smoke outside Buckingham Palace and nobody gives a shit. But because I was smoking outside the Quartermaster Store, then that is obviously a hanging offence and all hell breaks loose. I was about to find out, that everything I had done and learnt in civi street was now worth nothing. You will learn the army way, and if you don't then you're out.

There was about hundred and twenty men of all ages attending this three day selection process, which was being held in a small military establishment at Sutton Coalfield in Birmingham UK. I don't know how often these selection processes take place but I was now starting to understand the reason why the Recruitment Officer was in a hurry, to get me a rail warrant, so I could get the train to Birmingham. Perhaps they happen every three or four months, but I was just glad to be here, and most likely, I would have changed my mind on joining the army, if I had had to wait.

We were given a set of coveralls and an ashtray each, which was issued from the QM Stores and then shown to our rooms. The rooms could sleep eight men, and each room had four bunk beds, two tables with eight chairs, and eight lockers, and that was it. But it was only for two nights and so it was not a problem.

But I did have a problem, while everyone else was taking out there washing kit, towels, spare pants and socks, clean T shirts, I was signing a piece of paper saying that my bedding was clean and not soiled. I never had anything to unpack; I didn't even have a bag. I was stood there in a baggy T shirt, cement dust all over my jeans, and a pair of docs which had seen better days. The only thing that I had that was clean was my Harrington jacket which I loved. I explained my problem to a member of the staff and was told that there was not a shop on the camp, and it was my responsibility to comply with the letter that was sent to you, and to bring what was required. Trying to tell this idiot that I had just signed the papers a few hours ago was falling on deaf ears. So I stood in front of the seven other lads who I had never met before, and asked if one of them could give me half of their soap, and does anyone have a spare towel, as if they are going to bring two towels for two nights. I had no chance in trying to get a tooth brush, but I had a chance in getting some toothpaste. I got the half a bar of soap, and this lad tore his towel in half for me. For cleaning my teeth I stuck out my finger in the mornings when I was at the washroom and this guy squeezed toothpaste onto my finger, and that was it I was sorted.

The selection process was over three days and two nights. The 1st day saw young men arriving at different times and getting issued with their coveralls and signing for their bedding. In the evening we went to the gym, where a basic fitness test was conducted. You had to do a minimum of six pull ups, and ten sit ups. Then we had to do the standing jump test. You would wet your fingers, and with your arm stretched above your head, you would jump as high as you could, and touch the board with your fingers. We also had to complete a step test, and this involved stepping up onto a gym bench, and then stepping off of it again, you would do this for five minutes, and then one of the staff would take your pulse. The pulse checking would be repeated every minute for five minutes, apparently it's to check how quick your heart rate gets back to normal.

The following day would comprise of lectures, and a number of films, followed by an interview with one of the staff, I prayed I would not get the cigarette loony. That evening you would be told if you were successful or not, and also where and when you were going to do your training. Then the following morning your bedding would be checked for any piss stains, you would then hand back your coveralls and ashtrays, to the high and mighty QM Stores, and then as in my case get the train to where ever I was going.

After having breakfast we were told to get outside the accommodation block and form up in three ranks, well we managed three fairly straight lines, which all had a dog leg in them but we tried. We then walked over to a large hall, and that morning we listened to many lectures about the Army, and generally what life is like once you are serving, and are you prepared for this.

After lunch we were in our three crooked lines, and were waiting for a member of the staff to take us over to the hall, so we could continue with the lectures and the films. While we were waiting I lit up a cigarette and was happy puffing away, when out of the blue a member of the staff appeared. Everyone else was taken back over to the hall except me, I was told to stand with my feet together, with my arms down by my side and not to move, as he will be back in fifteen minutes. He was indeed back in fifteen minutes, but only to tell me to stand with my feet apart and put my arms behind my back. This went on for about one hour, when he finally told me to go to the hall, which I did hoping that I could still see some of the films.

I opened the outside door and got to the hall door where I could hear someone talking, I opened the door slowly so I could just slip in unnoticed which I managed to do, but there was no empty chairs nearby for me to sit on, so I just sat on the edge of the stairs. Then to my amazement the person who was talking said "ok that's it go away and make your three choices and good luck". I just sat there and watched everyone else stand up and start to leave the hall, they were saying things like, oh I fancy doing this, but I think that would be a better job, and that one's crap I am not doing that. Not doing what, and what would be better I was asking my roommates, but none of them really wanted to talk, because they were trying to decide what they wanted to do in the Army.

Tapping a chewed up pen between my teeth, and thinking what I wanted to do in the Army was not good for my brain; it was in overdrive but was not going anywhere. There were many posters on the walls, but one stood out from the others. There was a large truck with ammunition on the back of it, and the words Royal Corps of Transport. That was it that was what I was going to do, I was going to DRIVE. I would drive the trucks with all the stores on board, up to the men who were on the front line. The Royal Corps of Transport my mind was made up, and that was going to be my three choices and I was not going to change my mind.

Then it was my turn for the interview, and in I went, and then I had ten minutes trying to convince this seasoned soldier, that all I ever wanted to do was drive big Army Trucks and nothing else. That evening we were sat in our rooms chatting between ourselves wondering how we had done. We would be called into an office one by one and would be told our fate. It was like a doctor's surgery, people where going in worried and the majority were coming out happy, a few of the lads never got what they wanted but so be it. Then my name was called out and in I went, I don't know if I was looking worried, but I came out beaming and grinning from ear to ear. I had got into The Royal Corps of Transport Yippee.

Nobody got much sleep that night, we were all chatting about, what we were going to do, and where we were going to go for our training. After breakfast we handed back the kit we had been given, and our bedding was checked, it was then back over to the hall again. There was a long line of tables, and you moved along them like a conveyer belt, and by the time you got to the end you had in your possession, (your 8 figure Military Number that would be yours forever, a bus warrant, and a rail warrant, and in my case it was for Aldershot, and my first of many Military packed lunches).

CHAPTER FIVE

Having arrived in Aldershot sometime on Friday afternoon, I made my way to Buller Barracks which was going to be my home for the next six months. I was taken to the Guardroom and told that I was living in Kerr block ground floor and your name is on one of the doors. "Be at the Quartermasters Store at 1800hrs to be issued with your military uniform and equipment do you understand," "yes I replied," "yes what," "yes I understand," "yes corporal he shouted back at me do you understand", "yes corporal" I answered, and was then told to fuck off! out of the guardroom.
Well that was a nice reception, I thought as I was looking for my accommodation and when I found it I was quite impressed. There was my name on the door along with three others, and there were a lot of people moving around, they all seemed to know what they were doing, and nobody was interested in me. There was an empty bed in the corner of the room which was obviously mine. The three other beds had sheets and bedding already on them. There were pairs of boots on the table, and the smell of burnt polish, a smell of which would accompany me throughout my Army career.
Sign here said the store man, and remember if you lose any of your kit you will have to pay for it understand. Not knowing whether to say yes Corporal or ok mate I just mumbled and signed. Picture the scene, a single mattress folded, 2 x pillows 2 x sheets, 4 x blankets, 1 x bedspread, 2 x denim trousers, 2 x combat trousers, 2 x combat jackets, 2 x jumpers, 4 x shirts, 4 pairs of socks, 2 pairs of brand new boots, 1 x beret, 1 x green Sausage Army Holdall, 2 x towels, 1 x bed side locker made of wood, 1 x ashtray and a china mug, plus a few more other items. All of this was balancing on top of each other and I was being told to pick it up and take it away. I needed a fork lift to carry all this, but no such luck it was just me and my arms.

A lot of the lads had been in barracks for a few days, and some had even been here a week already, and all there kit was ready for the big day which was Monday the thirteenth of September 1976. That was the day we started our training and I had just two days to try and get ready, and look the part. I had signed up at the recruiting office on Tuesday the 7/9/1976 and had been to Birmingham and back, and now I had forty eight hours to get ready for my first ever parade. I burnt the candle both ends that weekend and with some help and advice from the others I was ready to go.

The time 0730 hrs. And we are all stood outside in three crooked lines and I looked a bag of shit. I had taken some advice on how to soften boot leather. I had stood in a bath of water for an hour or so, and when the leather had dried it was as hard as concrete and not pleasant on the feet. The crutch of my trousers was down to my knees, I had about two foot of shirt tucked into my trousers, and with the top button of my shirt done up, there was still enough room for another neck. The military jumper has elbow pads fitted on the arms, but the jumper was too big for me, so my elbow pads were on my wrists. My beret with the cap badge 1 inch above the left eye was so big that a helicopter could have landed on it. But I was proud I had made it on parade, even though I was a mess. In fact all of us were looking like a bag of shit, so I didn't feel too bad and now the long learning curve had just begun.

CHAPTER SIX

The training was to last for nine weeks, and on completion you would be granted one week's leave, and on your return you would start the Driver Training phase of your training. On passing your basic driving test you would then go onto the heavy goods driver training side and when you have passed that, you would then get posted to a working unit.

Basic training was hard both mentally and physically for us young recruits, but it had to be hard, they had to get the civilian way of life out of us and the military life drummed in. (As the saying goes they take out your civilian brain and input an Army brain). A typical day would be getting woken up by the staff banging the doors with a wooden pick helves, and shouting get up get up "hands of cocks get them on your socks" stand by your beds. You literally had seconds to get up and stand in your underpants by the side of your bed, sometimes with a semi on, but that soon went when they burst into the room.

If everybody was not up or actually stood by their beds, then press ups would begin for everyone in that room, so we all made sure we were up and stood by our beds. This was what the training staff wanted to instill into us, it was team building, and they wanted you to be working as one, and not as individuals. Plus who wants to do press ups at 0530hrs.

We were then to get washed and shaved, at least 90% of us never had a hair on our face but we had to shave. The washrooms looked like a scene from the Silence of the Lambs; people were cutting chunks out of their faces. Some of the lads would shave with their shirt and jumper on, this was to save time and get longer at breakfast. After you had stuffed yourself with sausages, eggs, bacon, fried bread, beans, and a mug of tea, you went back and cleaned the whole block and your room and get ready for inspection at 0730hrs.

We would get outside and on parade for 0750hrs and following that, it was onto the square for two hours learning how to march as a squad, moving left and right, backwards and forwards, and stopping as one. Back to the room for 10 o'clock and you then had thirty minutes, to go to the Naafi and get a drink and a sandwich. You then got changed into your army sports kit and got back outside for 1030hrs. Then it was a quick hour and a half of physical training, if we were not in the gym then we were out running for miles.

Finally it was back to the room where you would get a quick shower, and then into your combat dress and straight over to the cookhouse for lunch.

We would be back outside for 1330hrs where we go to the armoury and collect our weapons, and carry out weapon and field craft training. Evening meal was at 1700hrs and you would eat like a horse, because you were so hungry. Then it was time to get your kit ready for the next day, study all of your notes you had taken during the day, and keep reading the training manuals, all to be done by 2230hrs when it was lights out.

People were dropping like flies as the weeks went on, the intake had started off with about forty five recruits, and we were now down to about thirty, after four weeks of training. The odd broken bone, a couple of pulled muscles, lots of aching joints, but it was the mental side of the training that was getting to those who had chucked it in. We were not allowed to leave the barracks at any time and the only day you had off was a Sunday. But you were that exhausted you couldn't do much, and you had to get your kit ready for Monday.

There was just five more weeks of basic training left, and for those of us that were still standing we would have the daunting task of doing a passing out parade in front our parents, girlfriends, and maybe for some their boyfriends. But there was a lot more work to be done before we could even think about that, and the training was to get a lot harder both mentally and physically.

At the end of the fifth week we would be going out on our first exercise and it was to last for two nights. We would be putting into practice all that we had learnt so far in our training. It was also a test of the individual's character, we were told that we would not get any sleep, and you would be pushed and pushed until you gave up. They were looking at getting rid of at least five to ten more recruits by the beginning of the sixth week. We sat in our 4 man rooms wondering what they were going to throw at us, and who were the people they thought may fail and get kicked off the training. Speculation was rife but I knew in myself that I was not going to be one of those leaving, and surely I can stay awake for a couple of days and nights. It's not going to be as hard as what they are saying, they are bullshitting they are just trying to scare us.

Friday morning arrived and after a huge breakfast double of what you would normally eat, we were outside with all our equipment, and our nice new shinny combat suits, and to be honest we did not look like raw recruits. Our clothes were fitting us now because we had all grown into them, putting on at least a stone or more and we had muscles be it small ones, but they were beginning to show on our arms, chest, and legs. The staff then turned up and when you looked at them big arms small waist tailored uniform, you were brought back to reality, and yes, we were still a bag of shit.

It had taken us ages to squeeze all the items of kit that had to be packed into our webbing and back pack. That was an exercise in itself, it took us ages to do this and a few of us cheated. I could not get my towel into a certain pouch; you would actually have difficulty in fitting a flannel into it. So I cut it in half and never packed any soap, what was the point we were not going to get any rest, and the chance of having a wash was very slim. The other thing I never packed was my spare combat suit. What's the hard ship of living for three days in one set of combats, not a problem? So with all that extra room I had made, I packed all the sweets that the lads had brought, in fact I was now the mobile shop.

"Stand in a straight line and empty the contents of all your webbing and place it in front of you NOW". I said to the guy next to me their fucking joking, it took me hours to pack all this, and that was with me leaving kit out. They walked up the line and just by glancing down they could see if everything was there. I was about half way up the line and they were already shouting and bollocking people, and giving them the mandatory press ups to do. These lads that were doing press ups actually had all there kit, so what were they going to do to me. Well it did not take too long to find out, as the intake sergeant made his way up the line, when he just stopped and looked down at my clothing and equipment that was next to this mountain of sweets and cigarettes. He never said a word he didn't have to, just the presence of him being there was enough to make you literally shit yourself.

Standing at about 6ft 6inches tall and weighing about fourteen stone and at least a day's walk across his chest, and the fact that he was a mad Scotsman he didn't have to speak, he just glared at me. By now the blood had drained completely out of my body and my heart rate was of the scale. He then spoke "what is this" I opened my mouth and tried to make a noise, but all that came out was a high pitched note, followed by nothing, I had lost the basic art of speaking. The sergeant started to walk away but came back like a raging bull, and put his right foot straight threw all of my kit and sent it into space. I had moved back at least a foot in shock and in fright. By now this demented Scotsman had managed to spread all my kit over an area of about twenty square metres. He started shouting out "I like sweeties, sweeties for the sergeant, sweetie's everywhere I like sweeties". I was thinking he has gone fucking mad and that meant one thing, I was dead.

A couple of his minions picked up the sweets, and put them into a pile for the lunatic to most likely eat later. I will make an example of you Osborne on the exercise and he turned away and left. We were ordered to repack our kit and get into the back of the vehicles. So half of the intake never had their kit checked, and the kit I hadn't packed was not noticed, apart from the loss of all those sweets, and cigarettes, it wasn't that bad at the end of the day.

CHAPTER SEVEN

I was getting to know how a chip felt in a bag when it is getting shaken about so we can put salt and vinegar on them. Because that was how it felt in the back of the truck that was taking us to the exercise area. The driver was hitting every hole that was actually possible, and he never gave a shit about his cargo. It was raining and pretty cold well we were in the middle of October and in the UK that is the start of winter. The vehicle came to a sudden stop and we were ordered out of the truck and to get fell into 3 ranks. We were off on a five mile march, carrying full kit on our backs, and at a pace that an Olympic runner would train at. It never took long for a few of the lads too start struggling, and that was the cue for the instructors to start ranting and raging. You worthless pieces of shit, the government are wasting their money on you fuckers now move and catch up.
I was up with the main body of men, and there was no way on earth was I going to drop back and give them the satisfaction of seeing me struggling. Head down I wasn't even thinking, just keep going one foot in front of the other trying to ignore all the abuse the staff were giving us. We arrived at an area where there was a couple of tents and two land rovers, and the smell of food. We were breathing through every hole the body had, and I just wished god had made more holes, so I could get more air into my lungs. The lads were strung out over a large distance, and even though I was hurting all over and soaked I strangely felt good, because I had finished with the main body. Is Osborne here, oh no it's the mad jock Sgt "yes Sergeant" I answered, well at least my voice was back but for how long? Good well done everyone, and you Osborne and that was it he just walked away. Had he enjoyed all those sweeties and forgot all about the earlier incidents, maybe.
We were then given our orders and a scenario that was to cover the next two days, and then it was of into the trees where we started to put into practice, everything we had been taught so far in our training. With a pick and shovel we set about trying to make a two man trench 6ft x 2ft x 4ft. The staff were nowhere to be seen so we were left to our own devices which weren't much. After about half an hour of digging blisters had formed and popped, and were forming again on my hands. My arms were just burnt out and my head was spinning, and the best bit of all we had dug down only about 18inches. We kept looking over at the others to see how they were doing, and they were all pretty much in the same boat, but a

couple of trenches were looking good. Shit come on mate we can get this done, but we were digging on a bunch of tree roots, that had been there years, and they were not going to give up their place in this wood easily. Every time you would strike down onto the roots with the pick or shovel, you got a shooting pain through the hands and up the arms. But so did everyone else so it was a case of getting on with it.

Night time had arrived and everything was silent, no more digging, no noise, and no lights what so ever. Half standing half sitting in your trench pitch blackness all around you, you're cold, tired, and hungry, and knowing that the staff were out there and could attack you at any time, was not everyone's idea of having fun. The staff came around to check on us and bollocked all of us for the pathetic attempts we had made on our trenches. Every single noise would put you on edge, and you would be wide awake for the next 5 minutes, then you would drift off again into the land of nod. This was only an exercise, and the enemy was not real, and you know you're not really going to get shot.

There were four huge explosions, and gun fire was coming from all directions. My heart was racing and I was staring into darkness, I never had a bloody clue what was going on, and more importantly I didn't know what to do. So I just did what everyone else was doing, I grab my kit fired of a few rounds, and then run around like an idiot trying to get away. I must have run into at least half a dozen trees, I was getting stabbed in the face and neck plus I nearly swallowed a twig. Your clothes were getting caught on branches and the stupid helmet we had to wear was falling over your face all the time. I was moving around like a mummy, my arms were outstretched trying to feel my way through this wood, and I was nearly in tears as I was convinced, that the lunatic Scotsman who had said he would make an example of me was not that far behind. God I was shitting myself and was no longer tired or cold.

I carried on stumbling through the woods, when I realised that everything seemed to go very quiet. There was no more firing, no more explosions in fact there was no noise at all, so I crouched down and waited. I was by myself, and now had no idea where the rest of the troops were. Perhaps they had all got caught and were now in the middle of getting a major bollocking, at least I had made it away without getting caught. Osborne where are you? In you come. That's the end of this phase of the exercise, come on regroup, it was the screaming Jock. I just got even lower to the ground, there was no way was I going to answer him, it was a trap ha ha, and he can't fool me so I never said a word. Again and again he was calling me and each time his voice was getting more and more impatient; "get your fucking arse to me now Osborne or your history". I still hid but I started thinking, is he serious has this phase finished or not. But on hearing the anger in his voice I decided to break cover and shouted out I'm over here

Sergeant.
Dawn had started to break by now, and all I could focus on was this large object crashing through the trees, and heading straight towards me. He was yelling and screaming at the top of his voice, and unless you were Scottish, you had no idea what he was saying. Do I run and hide again because if I stay here I am going to die, too late he was there, and inside my face in fact he was inside my brain. I was finding it hard to keep my footing as I was being dragged sideways by my collar. He released his hold on me when we got back to the others, and I sat on the floor with the rest of the lads. I was trying to get my breath back, and also answer their questions like where have you been?, are you ok?, I was still feeling good with myself as I had not got caught.

The staff went over the last twenty four hours and gave good constructive criticism, which made a change from the constant bollockings that we were used to. We were given our 24 hr. ration packs and told to go and cook your breakfast, and to change out of your wet clothes. Well that was going to be interesting for me to do, as I only had 1 pair of combats and so I stayed in my wet clothes and cooked my breakfast. With the staff helping and showing us what to do, breakfast turned out to be all right, but then again it was the first food we had had for twenty four hours. We then had to get onto the track for an inspection, and were told of the day's activities. Out he came throwing the tent flap back and standing there like a god and starring at all of us, just him being here on the exercise made it a hundred times worse than what it already was. Then he started walking over in our direction, holding a rifle in one hand and a mug of tea or coffee in the other, and the facial expression of one pretty pissed of man.

One of you fuckers has lost something haven't you, I instinctively gripped my rifle even though I was already holding it but I had to check. The unfortunate person stepped forward and the heavens opened up on him, and then onto the rest of us as well, we were off tabbing again, head down and marching flat out. The staff was once again reminding us that we are a team and must work as one unit, and that means looking after each other. All those who had changed into their spare dry combats, were now exactly the same as me wet. I felt I had got away with not bringing spare clothing out with me; in fact I was quite smug about it.

A good couple of hours on the ranges followed by lunch things didn't seem too bad even the sun was out smiling. Field craft was next and we were to put into practice all that we had been taught i.e. judging distances, patrolling, concealment etc. We were given an eight figure grid reference, and were told that is where your rations have landed, and if you do not find them then you will all go hungry.

The light was starting to fade and it was getting colder, when we came to a large opening. We had to cross this area so we formed an extended line and broke from our cover, and immediately we were fired upon. Now the immediate action is (Dash, Down, Crawl, Sights Observe, and engage if you see the enemy.) Well that's what I done, I dashed forward a couple of steps, but when it came to the down and crawl part, I ran on a bit further because there was a huge puddle in front of me. Stop everyone go back let's do it again. So we did and we got hit again at the same place and I ran around the same puddle. Stop back you go and this time it was the sergeant who was giving the orders. We then started for the 3rd time and yes we got hit in the same place, but the only difference was that the lunatic Jock was standing directly on the other side of this large puddle and watched me run around it for the third time.

Everyone was ordered over to the puddle and the sergeant asked me "what do you do Osborne when you come under enemy fire". So I told him and I knew exactly what he was getting at when he said "why didn't you get down after you had dashed forward". Because the water was there sergeant and I thought if I ran around the puddle then I would get a better fire position. I was quite impressed with my answer but the mad jock was not impressed. You don't get paid to think Osborne you do as your told, so get over there and show us all how to crawl.

So I lay on the ground and crawled into the puddle. The water poured down the front of my clothes and it was freezing, within seconds I was submerged holding my head up like a turtle and edging forward on my elbows as I made my way towards the Sergeant. I went to get up but was told to stay there and he started talking, more like preaching a sermon. He then asked me how does one break cover Osborne. You never break cover, at the same point you went to ground, and you always roll left or right then get up. Well done Osborne now show us how it's done. So I took a deep breath and I rolled over and the water rushed into my ears, and up my nose, my helmet had moved from the top of my head and was hanging to one side, half full of water and up I got and moved forward.

Carry on with your objective, let's go and he was gone, that was all he said. Night had fallen and there was a strong cold wind blowing into our faces I was frozen and it didn't matter, what any of the others were saying to me. I hated that man and I hated the army, I wanted out and I wanted it there and then. We found our food and was told by the staff to make camp in some wooded area, there is no digging, no lights, just put up your ponchos and stay awake, there could be enemy activity tonight. Every bit of my clothing was wet and even though the others offered me some dry clothing I was stubborn, I didn't hate the Sergeant or the army anymore, I hated myself for trying to be a smart arse, and trying to beat the system. What a wanker I had been, and now I was paying for it but I was determined to get through the next couple of days. We ate the food cold but could only eat the lunch and the evening meal part of it, this comprised of cold fatty

sausages, and cold chicken curry with dry biscuits, some of the lads even eat their breakfast, but I saved mine and just as well .
The staff came into our area and after being correctly challenged they looked at our shelters, and our defensive positions and they seemed pretty happy with everything. The Sergeant found me facing outwards looking into the darkness for an invisible enemy, "how are you Osborne", fine sergeant, "have you eaten yet Osborne", yes Sergeant, "anything left Osborne" yes Sergeant my breakfast, "show me" so I did "well done Osborne carry on". I was chuffed to bits with myself, and I dared to think the Looney jock was quite impressed as well. I was freezing that night I just couldn't warm up; I would have been warmer sitting there naked, but you never knew when you would get attacked.
Morning came and we had not been attacked, so I dug a small hole and put my burner inside of it and put a brew on. A lot of the lads were still sleeping and I would have been as well had it not been for these wet clothes on my back. With half my brew drunk, I then started to cook my breakfast. Bacon grill and chocolate porridge heated up is so tasty; once it was cooked I lay under the poncho and had just started eating it, when the staff came over. They were challenged correctly but went into a fit when they saw people sleeping and no camp routine was getting done i.e. cleaning weapons, eating, and so on so on. "Everyone get fell in "yelled the Sergeant so I grabbed my kit and stood in line with the others, people were forgetting there webbing, some turned up without their weapon, these individuals were dealt with, by doing push-ups.
Go and get your breakfast Osborne and bring it here, how did he know I had cooked my breakfast I thought if he had smelt the cooking it could have been anybody's. So I doubled away, and returned with my mess tins, with my half eaten breakfast and my mug of tea. I stood in front of him, and was just waiting for my breakfast to go airborne. I don't want your breakfast Osborne get fell in with the rest and carry on eating. Well to say I was shocked would be lying, so there I was eating my porridge and bacon grill, and all the time the sergeant was ripping into the rest of the lads. It was very hard not to smile but inside I was beaming. No one else had cooked that morning and they were not going to either as everyone had to put all their remaining food in front of them and the staff came along and took it all away. We were told to pack up all our kit and be ready on the track in thirty minutes. That was the end of the exercise, and I must admit they were the best words I had heard all weekend.
Safely back in camp and sitting under the drill shed we started to clean our weapons, and this would take ages. But when it was passed clean by one of the staff, you were free to go to your billet and get your kit ready and sorted out for Monday. After about 5 attempts of thinking that my weapon was clean I was finally told to go and hand it in.

CHAPTER EIGHT

Just four weeks to go and half way through the training, and the numbers where still falling, and they were just about to get a lot worse. After the Monday morning inspection we were all sat in the classroom waiting for the staff to give us a debriefing on the exercise. With the debriefing over and all the points noted, I actually believe the staff were quite happy with our performances. The officer in charge of our intake was a young Lieutenant, we never saw much of him, but he was here today to ask the question is there anyone here who does not want to be here? Silence, and then a hand went up, followed by three others, I was surprised with one of the lads who wanted to quit, but talking to him later on I understood why. He was a bit older than me and was married with a child, and he missed his wife and child so much he decided to get out.

The sixth and seventh week was pretty much the same, lots of marching with and without weapons, weapon training, including live firing with the 9mm pistol; this was not our personnel weapon, we were just lucky to get the chance to fire it. Lots more fitness training including the assault course, and more in-depth field craft training. Things were getting better by the day, instead of the constant bollockings; we were actually given a bit more slack and a little bit of freedom. End of week seven and another 72hr exercise was coming up and this time I made no mistakes. I checked over and over again and made sure that I had every bit of kit that was required. The loony sergeant was becoming more approachable and on a couple of times he was funny, but they were few and far between.

The exercise was physically demanding with very little sleep, so mistakes were bound to be made and they were, but it's better to do the mistakes now, while in training then do them in a real combat situation. I made a mistake and it involved the Lieutenant who was out with us on this exercise. I was on dead man stag, this is a term used through the military and it means during the hours of 0200-0500 you are the ears and eyes of the unit. While everyone is catching some zzzz you are in your hole trying to keep awake, you are as tired as the rest but its tuff shit if that's the stag you have pulled.

My stag finished at 0500hrs and after being relieved I was to wake up the Troopy (Lt) not a problem. Stag finished I made my way over to where he was sleeping and started to whisper, Sir Sir its five o'clock, no answer in fact no movement. I then whispered again Sir Sir and this time I pushed his sleeping bag, and he came out of his sleep and said "who's this". "It's me Sir it's your early call", who's me came the answer, well he asked so I told him,

I said its Ossie Sir. Well fuck my sainted aunt he went from someone, who was asleep a few seconds ago, to a maniac who wanted to pull my head off. He couldn't get out of his bag, thank fuck, but that only infuriated him even more. With all the noise that he was making the other staff were woken up, including the mad jock who was asking what's going on. We are not on first name terms Osborne, and we are not related thank God shouted the Lt who was still tangled up in his bag. "Whose not related Sir" said the Sergeant? That was it I was straight back to my trench, wide awake and waiting for my name to be bellowed out across the exercise area, but it never was. Later that morning the Sergeant did walk by me with a smirk all over his face, and as he passed he said in a low voice "ITS OSSIE SIR" and chuckled and walked straight on by. The incident was not mentioned again on the exercise but it would come up later on at the end of the training.

CHAPTER NINE

The final week of the training had arrived, and it was mainly geared around the Passing out Parade which was to take place on the Friday Afternoon. This was our chance to show our parents and all the training staff, that nine weeks ago, we were civilians who knew very little if anything about the army. Now nine weeks later we knew a lot more, and at least we could march as a squad, and we had come together as a team. I had learnt so much about myself be it mentally or physically and most importantly how to be a team member. Having the confidence to stand up and talk in front of strangers or even friends was never a problem for me, but for some of the lads it was a right problem. It was drummed into you everyday Confidence, Confidence, Confidence, you have to have the confidence in your own abilities, and you need to show those abilities when the opportunities arise.

During the exercise phases of our training we were all given different tasks to do, i.e. lead a patrol from one point to another point, carry out a recon patrol, or even being the Troop Commander. All of these tasks would have involved you showing off your leadership skills, and most of all showing that you have the confidence to lead. From day one I can honestly say that I loved it. I looked at the training as a personal challenge, and I was not going to fail, and it never crossed my mind to ask to leave the army.

There were seventeen of us left out of the original forty something that had started. Nearly half had fallen by the way side, and to be part of the seventeen gave me such a great feeling of achievement and proudness. Dress rehearsal after dress rehearsal, we knew the moves inside out but as they say practice makes perfect, and who wants to cock up on the final day no one. Our No2 Dress uniforms were immaculate, and highly pressed and fitted us like a glove. When you put it on you grew two inches in height because you felt so proud to wear it. In later years the proudness wore of and it was a pain to wear the bloody things but that's another story.

During the training I had been awarded the trophy for the best shot in the intake and would receive the trophy during the passing out parade. My name would be called out but only this time it wasn't for a bollocking, and I would have to march forward by myself to the Brigadier come to a halt and salute him. I would then receive my medal, salute again, do an about turn and march back and take up my place within the ranks. For some reason this was playing on my mind why I do not know, but it was a concern and I was worried about it. The day before the parade I asked if it was possible to speak to the mad Scotsman a personal one on one was that possible.

Eyebrows were raised because no one knew what it was about.
What is it Osborne? "well Sergeant I am," "don't stand in the fucking door way you're not a door, even though your head is made of wood what's up". I explained that I was worried about going forward to receive my medal. Sitting back he said "why on earth are you worried, after all you have done this should be a piece of cake for you".
You tried taking sweets and fags out on an exercise which was against my orders, you only took one set of combats with you on the first exercise, and you never moaned once about being wet for three days, and you even tried to get on first name terms with the Troop Commander. And you're worried about meeting an old Brigadier, who doesn't even know you, and most likely will forget he was even here after a week or two, now piss of I'm busy. Well that done the trick he was right, I had played the system and at times rode my luck, but I was still here so I must have done something right.
The band struck up and marched onto the Square and took up their positions five minutes to go final checks, fags out, ready to go. Let's have a good one shouted the Sergeant and onto the square we marched. Leaning back slightly at the waist with my rifle in my left hand, and sitting perfectly still in the shoulder, I was swinging my right arm shoulder high, and the adrenalin was pumping through my body. The band was blasting out some tune that only band people could name, and as we turned onto the square I could see all the families sitting there out of the corner of my eye. The feeling was fantastic and in fact my eyes started to fill up, but that was down to the moment, the adrenalin, and the sheer delight of passing the training. The mums and dads were taking pictures of their sons, some were even waving, as if they were going to wave back to them, but they were obviously so proud of their sons. The occasion had got to a few of the parents and there was the odd handkerchief being used.
I was in the front rank and 2nd from the right, but during training I wished I was in the rear rank, so if I made a mistake nobody would notice. But I would not give up my position for anything now; I wanted to be there right in the front. Over the next 45 minutes we carried out a number of rifle exercises, and marched around a bit which the crowd loved. Any nerves you had had were long gone, we were showing off well I was and I'm sure the rest were as well.
The band were moving to another area on the square and the Sergeant was walking passed the front rank telling us all, that we were doing a good job and to keep it up. He stood in front of me and said, "He won't remember he has been here in a week's time" he then grinned and took up his place to the right of the intake. Here we go Ossie your next and don't fuck it up. I couldn't believe what I had heard the Sergeant had called me Ossie, WOW I was in shock. Then my name got called and out I went in front of

everyone. I remember looking at the Brigadier when he gave me my trophy and thinking god the Sarge is right I wonder if he will remember this in a week's time.

We done a final march pass and saluted the Brigadier and all those who were watching us, who by the way were all standing and cheering. Some were even shouting out there sons names hi John I'm here, over here David coo wee, they were enjoying it and so were we. Out of site and behind the drill shed we started to hug each other, we had done it, we had completed nine weeks of bullshit and now it was over. The fags came out and each one of us got a beer which I drank straight down and then it was back to the square to meet the mums and dads.

My parents were not there, they were not even aware that I had joined the army, and just completed my training, yes it was a bit sad and lonely at the time but I was chatting to the other mums and dads, so it wasn't that bad. But I knew one man who was watching and that was my granddad, he would have been so proud of me.

CHAPTER TEN

After a well-deserved one week's leave we had all returned back to camp, refreshed and with a spring in our steps. I was feeling full of myself as I passed the sentry on the gate and started to amble up the road to my accommodation. I was looking at the square where I had spent many an hour in all weathers, and not forgetting the assault course where I had felt like dying many times. But that was all in the past, I had done my training and now I was a soldier. Get your fucking arms up shoulder high you piece of shit, swing those fucking arms or I will be swinging you. My arms shot up and I was marching again, (that's better) came the voice with no face. I never did find out who was bollocking me but it done the trick, I was back in the land of the living again.

My kit was ironed and I was ready for Driver Training, which started on Monday morning, and the best thing about it was I only had to brush polish my boots. No more sitting up in the early hours of the morning, trying to make them look like glass. It felt strange standing outside the Dvr Trg Wing, knowing that we were now going to be taught to drive by civilians. This was going to be strange, how do you work with civvies, is it still YES SIR, NO SIR, RUN AROUND SIR.

On hearing your name being called out, you broke ranks and went over and met your instructor, you then completed a bit of paper work and away you went. My name was called out and over I went to meet my instructor, who was a female. Oh no! What have I done to deserve this, a women driver and to make it worse a women instructor. Hi Steven how are you, um um that was all that came out, how chilled out can someone be. I was taken aback by her approach and now I was glad that I had got a women instructor.

Most of the driving instructors in the MOD were and are still ex-Military personnel. I have always said that these people, who do this type of work, are too scared to break away from the Army, and experience life by working in Civilian Street, but these people would disagree with my thoughts. I explained to the lady instructor that I had drove before and I knew where and what the pedals were for, but no we started from the very beginning (there's a song in there somewhere).

After only eleven hours of Dvr Trg I was put in for my test, this was only Thursday morning three days had passed and here I was with my instructor waiting for the examiner. I wasn't nervous I was full of confidence, and besides what can civilians do to you, I had just survived nine weeks of basic training. This was how I was to think for the next twenty three years, the Army had alienated me against the civilian population.

I had a great drive and when I finished the examiner asked a couple of questions on the Highway Code and said "I am pleased to say you have passed". Seventeen years old and a driving license, and next week its HGV Training things cannot get any better or can they.

What am I going to do with myself on my day off; I will just have a lay in and chill WRONG. Osborne you're on kitchen duty tomorrow you are to report to the cook house at 0700hrs. But I'm on Dvr Trg, know you're not, you passed your test this morning and congratulations Osborne, just make sure you're not late. This was not right I had passed my test and yet I was up and out before the others were even waking up. And to make matters worse I was going to be scrubbing pots and plates all day, my Wimpey bar days had come back to haunt me.

I had a great day in the cook house, I had finished the pots and pans by 0930hrs then I had free time until twelve o'clock. I was out of the cook house by two in the afternoon and it was free time again. Another couple of hours in the evening and that was me done. The good thing about working in the cook house is that you can eat whatever you wanted. I was picking all day, and I must have consumed about 20 sausages without a problem while I was there. This was the start of an eating disorder that lasted all my Army Career. I would eat about five sausages in the morning and the same again for lunch and tea. In the years that followed I would walk past the cook house when on exercise, and could not stop myself from pinching a sausage.

My instructor for the HGV phase of my Dvr Trg was a complete opposite to the lady who had taught me to drive. He was large very large and would sweat a lot even though we were in December and he just loved to have the heater on full. With an instant dislike to this man my army brain came into action (These are civilians working for us the army) so the window would come down and the heater off, I even told him that I felt like passing out as it was too hot. But he was great after that, you see a man that size needs to eat and doesn't want to work too hard, so our daily routine would be something like this.

Start to drive at 0830hrs a bit of maneuvering around i.e. reversing around some cones up at the Dvr Trg Area, and then it was off to a small cafe on the Guildford bypass which would be packed with other Dvr Trg vehicles. Arrive there at about 1030hrs and get a burger and a mug of tea. We would stay there until about 1130hrs, then it was a bit more driving and back to camp for 1230 and lunch. I would meet him again at about 1400hrs where we would drive around until 1600hrs, when it was back to camp. I would then give the vehicle a quick wash down and would normally get away for 1630hrs.

This routine went on for a couple of weeks and then I was put in for my HGV test. It was raining very hard and the examiner wasn't looking too pleased, I was thinking trust me to get a miserable bastard but into the truck he climbed and of we went. The examiner is meant to get out of the vehicle while you are carrying out the forward and reversing maneuvering phases of the test. But there was no way, was this guy even thinking about leaving the comfort of the cab not a chance. During the reversing stage of the test, you have to maneuver the vehicle into a small area, and stop with the rear of the vehicle in a twelve inch space. If you go beyond the twelve inch space, or stop short of it then you would fail. The examiner would then go and check to see how you done. But not this one he looked in the mirror and said "how does that look", I answered "I think it's pretty good", "I agree well done drive on". I knew from that moment I would pass the test as long as I didn't drive into anyone or anything. Well done Steve you passed and thank you for a good drive, and good luck for the future. I said thank you very much to my instructor for getting me through my test and handed in my pass certificate into the transport office so it could get sent away, and get added to my car license.

CHAPTER ELEVEN

Christmas was approaching fast and I was looking at getting away for a couple of days, and maybe catching up with a few friends. The camp was starting to get quite now, what with people leaving and going on leave, plus there were no new intakes arriving so the camp had an air of normality about it. There was no screaming and shouting going on, the parade ground was empty, even the band were not practicing and making a racket. I had finished my training and was now just waiting for my first posting to come through, how long will it take, where would I be going, how long will I go there for, all these questions where running through my head.

Standing on parade and waiting to get told to hand in your bedding and go on leave for a couple of weeks never came; in fact it was the opposite. Myself and a few of the lads were told that we were to cover the Christmas Guard. What a kick in the crown jewels I had pulled guard duty on the 21st, 23rd, 25th, 27th, and the 29th and the days we were not on guard, we were on standby. Well I was right pissed off with everyone going away and saying have a good Christmas, Happy New Year, well at least I would not be working over the new year. Merry Christmas now piss off, and go home and enjoy yourselves you lucky bastards! wankers.! Those Ten days drifted by without any incident which was a good thing, but walking around the perimeter fence at three o'clock on Christmas morning with a pick handle and a torch sucks. What were we to do if someone tried to get in, shout at them, tell them to go away, what a load of bollocks but there you go. Last duty, last standby and I was finished it was New Year's Eve 1976/77 and I was at a loss. Do I go down town and have a beer, but this is a town full of hardened soldiers drinking gallons of beer and spirits and looking for a fight. Or do I just hang around with a couple of guys, get a few beers from the off license and get drunk. That sounded like a good idea so that's what we done, the party lasted for three days and it was great three days.

The camp was back to normal now with new recruits arriving daily getting ready to start their training, the Christmas and New Year break had come and passed. The shouting and screaming had started again, and of course the bollockings had started to be given out. I was still waiting for my posting and as I had completed everything in my training syllabus I was just hanging around trying to keep out of sight, so I would not get picked for guard duties or cookhouse fatigues.

Then it came through I was being posted to 38 Sqn RCT which was based in Mulheim ad Ruhr West Germany. I could not believe it, I was going to fly for the first time, and I was going to live in Europe. I was to report to my new unit on the 11th March 1977 and now I didn't care if I done cookhouse duties or any duties come to that, I was going to my first working unit.

Looking back at the training depot as the vehicle I was sitting in pulled out of the gates, I felt a sense of relief but also some sadness, why I don't know., I had been bollocked there daily, had my body changed forever. I had under gone a brain transplant, the young civilian one had been taken out and thrown away, and a fresh brand new military one fitted.

But with my shoulders back and chest out I boarded the plane and took my seat. Trying not to show my fear I clipped the seat belt together and just sat there. This middle aged man sat down and started talking to me, how can I concentrate on talking to this stranger, when I am very concerned about flying, but I managed to try and sound normal. "First time flying" he asked. "No I've flown loads of times mate, I'm just going back to Germany after being on leave I'm in the army." Not much else was said between us during the flight, he must have thought what a tit head, and he is meant to protect us God help us all.

CHAPTER TWELVE

The Telephone landed just yards from where I was standing, and the pavement was littered with the glass from the window which it had come through. A corporal was looking through the window frame which once held glass, and was shouting at the phone in a Scottish accent, oh no! not another mad jock, surely not. I found out later he was the sheriff of the camp, i.e. he was the SSMs right hand man, and was not impressed with the phone call, so in a fit of rage he hurled the phone through the window.
After being shown to my bed space which was in a four man room, I collected my bedding and started to unpack my things. The room was empty as the other 3 lads were at work, and I was wondering what my new room mates were like and it didn't take long to find out. The door flew open and in they came, wearing coveralls and stinking of paint and diesel, with their berets on the back of their heads. "Who the fuck are you NIG? (New in Germany) and what the fuck are you doing in here?." I told them that this is where I was told to come by a Sgt from the stores. A fucking red arse! "What's your name?" so I told them it was Ossie, and that stayed with me throughout my career. Do you drink said one of the lads who was lying on his bed in his stinking coveralls. He still had his beret on the back of his head, which was now squashed into the pillow, and a cigarette in his mouth. Yes I said "I have a few beers now and then", good then were of too the Naafi at seven o'clock be ready.
They then started to talk between themselves, fancy getting a fucking NIG in the room, why do we have to have him, and also what they were going to get up to that night. Each one of them had a stereo sat by their bed, and all three stereo systems were on playing different music loud, in fact it was so loud you could not have spoken to one another, not that they wanted to speak to me anyway.
The cookhouse was basically the same as the one I had just left in Aldershot; the only difference was that we used to line up and move along the hot plate in an orderly manner. Over here it was a free for all, I would go to get the spoon so I could get some beans, when someone else would reach around, or over me and would say wait, and this was what it was like. I remember walking along the hot plate and I could see a couple of chicken pies and thought that will do for my tea. There was only one left when I got there, and I was not going to risk losing a limb, for the sake of a chicken pie so I left it. This happened at breakfast, dinner, and tea and it did not take long to work it out. It was seniority, as simple as that, those who had served the longest in the army, thought they had this god forgiven right to jump

the queue, and in my eyes they did.

I was showered and ready for 7pm and sat on my bed waiting to go to the Naafi, two of the three lads were still asleep while the other one was reading a porn mag. He looked up and said "are you ready", yes I answered and he proceeded to wake up the other two. On waking up they just took their boots and coveralls off, put their jeans on, T shirts, and trainers, and said let's go.

The Naafi bar was pretty basic, it had chairs, tables, ashtrays, a few vending machines that were still packed with pies, and pasties, cartons of milk, and soft drinks. You're in the chair Nig so go and get the first round in, so up to the bar I went and waited for the bar maid to serve me. But she was too engrossed in a conversation with another customer. "Where's the fucking beers nig?, "just waiting to get served" I replied. Then one of the guys said to the bar maid serve the Red Arse will ya. Her reply was "if he stands there like a fucking tit and doesn't talk, how the fuck am I to know what he wants". Well I had learnt how to get food, and also how to order beer in a working unit. But I had a long learning curve ahead of me in mastering the art of drinking with these lads.

There was about twelve of us sitting in a group around a couple of tables, which were starting to get full of empty beer cans, when another can of beer was put in front of me. I did not want any more beers, so I said no thanks I am off, but as I stood up to go, I heard where the fuck are you going sit down and have a beer, you're ok. I was shit faced and the thought of more beer didn't seem a good idea, but I did as I was told and sat down. After some more beer and on the verge of passing out I made my way to the toilet and threw up, I was bouncing of the walls and I knew I had to get back to the room. So I leant against the wall and found my way out of the Naafi building, I managed to get down the stairs somehow without breaking my neck, and finally made it back to the safety of my room, where I collapsed on my bed and into unconsciousness.

CHAPTER THIRTEEN

The first three years of my army career and I believe everyone's career is a learning curve and you had to learn fast. You have to take the crap that you are given every day while you are at work. At the end of the day you still got all the shit, but the most important thing of all, you had to set your stall out and stand up for yourself. If you were the quite type and just agreed to do whatever you were told, then life was going to be bad for you. You also had to remember that you were the new kid on the block, and you knew nothing of what life was like in a working unit.

Like in all walks of life the new kid gets the crap, but it is different in the Army, the Army is your family and you cannot run to an outside agency for help. A punch in the face from another soldier is part of the learning curve, if you went running to a senior person and said I got hit by Pte Bloggs the answer would be, good you most likely deserved it now fuck off or I will punch you myself.

So you had to show what type of person you were, and if that meant saying no to somebody telling you to do his job, i.e. the cleaning of the toilets then so be it. Now if that meant getting into a fight over it then so be it that's what you had to do. This was the only way to get some respect from the SWEATS (these were people who had served 6 or more years' service).

While all this is going on you had the mammoth task of trying to learn the role your unit played in the bigger picture, and also what role you was expected to play. The first six months were pretty frantic, I took my HGV Class 2 test, and passed it and I was still 17 years of age. I also took a basic mechanics course, these were things you had to achieve others wise you were a waste of time to the unit and you would be posted out. So learning quick and showing others that you was not a stepping stone for people to walk on was very important and of course great fun.

Jokes are played on new kids all the time and there are a couple that will always make me smile. I was working on this vehicle and the front wheels had to come off so we needed axle stands to support the weight of the vehicle. But this particular time the guy I was working with asked me to go to the stores and ask for a LONG STAND so of I went. I asked the store man can I have a LONG STAND please, he said ok and walked away and left me standing there. Ten minutes goes by and I'm still there waiting, and the store man comes back and asks if I am ok, and off he goes again. Then the penny drops what a dick head I have been, yes it was a LONG STAND I was there for about 30 minutes. When I got back to the vehicle my boss was there and he bollocked me for walking off the job and for skiving.

Another one that will stay with me forever was the time I was asked to go to the paint store and get a small tin of tartan paint, as it was needed for a vehicle that was going to go to a Scottish unit. So of I went and asked the store man who went away apparently looking for it. I wasn't to know that he had been tipped of already and was playing along with the joke. He was great and made out he was looking for the tin of paint for at least twenty minutes and then finally told me what an idiot I had been to fall for a joke like that. You get so much stick from the lads, but it was all good fun, and it's part of the learning curve.

Going on exercises came thick and fast and it wasn't for a weekend, it would be two to four weeks at a time but you got used to it and they were great to be on. Nobody wanted to stay back in the camp when the majority of the Sqn was away on exercise, because you get all the shit jobs, you're not with your mates, and you feel left out and not part of the unit.

The vehicles we used to drive in the unit was mainly the AEC 10 Ton truck, this vehicle was so basic it was from the Jurassic days, there was no power steering so if you were turning at a slow speed you had to stand up. The top speed was 32 mph and if you got one that done 34 or 35 mph you were proud and told everyone. After driving one of these vehicles for a day you were physically knackered so it was up to the bar and have a few beers.

Drinking was part of the culture and every night the pigs bar was packed with thirty or more lads having fun and getting drunk. If you were driving the next day you would still go out drinking but only get half drunk well that was the idea. Monday to Sunday the bar would be packed and at the weekends the married personnel would come into the bar with their wives, and join in some of the drinking games that used to take place.

After a few beers it was common practice for someone to open up one of the bar windows, and stand on the window sill. He would then jump towards a large tree that was about 10 feet away from the window, and hopefully grab hold of the trunk and climb down. He would then return to the bar where he would get a round of applause and a free pint. Sounds easy!, well it was, but this particular weekend after a lot of beer we started doing it blind folded. Bearing in mind we were two floors up so it was more a case of bravado and not losing face then just doing it.

We had a new lad who had been with us for about one month and he thought he knew it all, and was having problems fitting in, so we invited him to do this jump, which he accepted with a cocky attitude. After blindfolding him we led him to a window, but this window had no tree outside. He jumped and his arms were waving around trying to grab the tree, whack straight into the ground ooh!. Squaddie humour is to laugh when people hurt themselves and that's what we did. We were laughing uncontrollably he was alive and just moaning, a broken arm and bruises and he was fine. As far as I am aware he was never told what really happened, but he changed his attitude straight away and became one of the family. But like everything else in this world there is always a serious side to life, and we were no different and it came in the form of Northern Ireland.

CHAPTER FOURTEEN

This was exciting times for myself and some of the new lads, but very much old hat too those who had been a couple of times before. We were flying out on 01 April 79 and it was not an April fool's joke either a lot had to be done before we could be deployed to NI. January, February, March would be flat out training (ranges, weapon handling, doing it blind folded, physical training every day, radio trg, patrolling in small teams, reacting to enemy fire, first aid,) and much much more. Even though it was hard it was great to be involved in something like this. Not everyone is able to go to Ireland, there has to be a rear party left behind to look after the day to day running of the camp. There was still the security of the camp that had to be looked after, and of course the welfare of the wives and children. Finally the list of all those going to Ireland was displayed and I was just so happy I was going and not one of those left behind on rear party.

Even though the trg was hard we still had a lot fun doing it. We would go down to Tin City for a week or two. Tin city was purposely built to resemble a small town. It had houses, gardens, roads, everything you would get in a town even a working bar absolutely brilliant. Accommodation was so so a bit small and cramped but that was what is was like out there, and the two weeks would be run as if we were in Ireland. I was out patrolling one night when we came under fire and believe me it takes a second or two to realise what's actually going on and then you are back in the real world. The patrol leader ordered us to do a follow up i.e. go toward the area where the shots had come from. So there we were running through gardens over walls taking cover behind whatever is available and breathing out of our arse. Feeling quite satisfied that we had done a good job and surrounded the house where the shot had come from we were brought back to earth with a bump. The senior trg staff Warrant Officer came over and informed us at the top of his voice, (that we had gone off in the opposite direction of where the contact was in other words we had run away).

Another occasion was when there was a mock riot. 40 or 50 other guys from a different unit would be the rioters and would throw bricks, petrol bombs whatever at us, this was to give us an indication of what to expect when we got out there. There is no love lost between different units in the Army, and these were Infantry lads and they were getting stuck in to us. Well as to be expected things got out of hand and before the trg staff could intervene a full blooded fight had broken out between 80 and 100 Squaddies. There were a few real injuries cuts, the odd tooth went missing, and a couple of broken noses but that's what happens.

The next time we had riot trg it was more closely monitored but the air was still very tense. With all the training completed we had a couple of days to relax with the family before we were of on our four months tour. Excited, nervous, upset, all these feelings were rolled into one and all you wanted to do was just get out there. With all my goodbyes said and the tears wiped away, and a final wave to my young wife and to my son who was going to have his first birthday in two days' time. I walked into the camp with all my kit, collected my personnel weapon and boarded the bus to the military airport. I was now on my way, and this was to be the first of many tours for me.

CHAPTER FIFTEEN

My head was going from left to right, looking up and looking back, my eyes darting side to side and my brain was trying to take it all in. Here I was in Northern Ireland, 19yrs of age, on my 1st tour of duty and if I was honest I was pretty scared for the first couple of days, but I had been trained for this and had to believe in myself no matter what. The people who had trained us have had so much experience in NI (been there and done it) you have to trust them and everything they had taught you.
We all arrived at the main camp and after all the administration was completed we all knew where we were going to spend our next 4 months. There were a number of units spread out around the Province that required RCT support. These would have been Infantry units, EOD units, and medical units. Personnel would join that unit and be under there command for the duration of their tour. I was to be working out of Moscow camp which was situated behind the famous Belfast docks. Our main role was to support all the units within NI with their logistic needs. Anything from food, fuel, medical stores, barbed wire, whatever was needed it was our job to transport it to them when required.
The accommodation was a large porta cabin with rooms inside. Each room was about 16ft long and 9ft wide and inside would be three double bunk beds, six metal lockers about a foot wide, a table and four chairs and that was it. So the six of us piled into this shoe box and fought over who would have the top bunks and which was the best locker. So you can imagine there was not much room for six soldiers and all there kit but we got in and sorted it out. One set of working clothes would be hanging up at any one time, because that's all there was room for, and if you used something from your bag, once you had finished with it you would put it away again nothing was ever left out. And following tradition every imaginable bit of wall space was covered with naked women from ceiling to floor, some of the pictures had seen better days, so we replenished the old with new. And finally the original door had been removed and was replaced with a number of cardboard boxes laid out like a door and masking taped together, different but it worked even though the door would bend slightly in the middle.
I saw my first Choggie shop in Moscow camp these were all over NI, if the army were there then the Choggies would be there. They were run by Indians and were open literally twenty four hours a day. The Choggie would live in a small building where they would have a cooker a fridge and a huge tea urn. We would come in from detail and it did not matter what time it was he would be there with his tea urn, and always offering to make you

egg banjos or sausage sarnies. The other thing the Choggie shop had was a Space Invaders machine the latest edition, and there were always lads in there waiting for a shot at it.

One morning all hell let loose at the choggie shop, Mr. choggie had got up and opened his door only to find someone had covered his outside door handle, and door in bacon, and slices of beef, to say he was pissed off would be an understatement. He threatened to leave and go elsewhere, and that would have been a disaster what no choggie. After a long chat with the SSM and thousands of apologies from different people he agreed to stay, but the bastard put his prices up a penny or two. The culprit was never found but we all had a good idea who it was.

There was also a disco every Wednesday and Saturday which to be honest was quite good. A 4 ton truck would go out and collect the girls from certain areas and bring them back to camp. The tail board would drop down and the girls would climb out the back of the truck in the best lady like way possible. The disco lasted until midnight when the girls would get loaded up again, but this time not in the best of lady like manner and get dropped off. Guys would be there as the truck was getting loaded getting hugs and kisses and saying see you on Saturday be good I LOVE YOU.

Some guys did fall in love and got married later on but others just went there for one thing to see if they could pull. Even though it was great to talk to the opposite sex and have a laugh you never really knew who you were talking to and where your conversation could end up. A simple thing like (well there are 4 trucks going to Derry tomorrow at 0800hrs) could lead to a major incident so you had to be careful in what you said. But overall it was a good laugh and gave some rest bite to the lads. And remember these girls took a risk as well, being seen coming out of an Army camp late at night and getting dropped off could seriously damage their health

CHAPTER SIXTEEN

After a few weeks had passed everyone knew the routes that we took like the back of their hand, there was four main routes used every day which took you all over the Province. Four trucks doubled manned and a guy sat in the back of the last truck, he was riding shot gun and this was mirrored on all the routes. The guy in the back would be watching out for any suspicious vehicles that could be following them, and if people were taking a lot of unusual interest i.e. taking photos, scribbling down things, basically anything that looked out of the ordinary. Stopping at traffic lights was a tense time as you were a sitting duck so the man in the back would have his weapon in the shoulder and would be scanning all the windows, doorways, anywhere that could conceal a shooter. You just never knew who was who, and where they could be hiding. We would get abuse from both sides "Catholics and Protestants" so we couldn't trust anyone and each one was as bad as the other.

One particular day we were on a foot patrol and it was chucking down with rain and the wind was biting into your body through the wet combat suits, we never had the wonderful thing called Gortex in those days. A girl came up to me I would say she was 10 years of age carrying a mug of coffee, she said here soldier and handed me the mug. After saying cheers I moved the mug from side to side and slopped out some of the coffee to see if anything else apart from coffee was in the mug, and there it was a used tampax which had been under a stone to hold it down. When I looked up there was a women at the door shouting and telling me where to go in no uncertain terms.

But we always got our own back I remembered the address and later that evening or should I say the early hours of the next day, a patrol would be out patrolling that area and I had already passed onto them what had happened that day. It was known in the army as the 4 o'clock knock. Everyone is asleep in the house when all of a sudden the door is booted in and there are soldiers in your house. After a five minute one way conversation with the head of the family the patrol would then leave the house hoping that they had got the message.

My R& R was coming up and that is when you go home for four days and see your family and just chill out. It's called Rest and Recuperation and after 3 months I was looking forward to it. The day came and after a quick flight I arrived back in Germany it was great seeing the wife again and my son and just chilling out doing normal things again. Even though it was only four days I could not help but keep thinking about the lads in Ireland and what was happening, and to be honest I missed not being there with them. It sounds sad but it's true I wanted to go back to Ireland I did not want to be here I felt I should be out there and not sat at home. Those last 2 days dragged and even though I never showed it I was glad to get into the transport and get taken to the airport so I could fly back to be with my other family.

Not much really happened in the last couple of weeks of the tour, normal details were being carried out, people being taken from A to B, and the wind down feeling was starting to set in. The final disco was upon us and god there was some tears at the end. There were promises of yes I will wait for you, phone me and I will fly over.

But the main thing was to get the camp ready for the hand over to the next unit that was to take over from us. The advance party had arrived, and when you see them you know you're in your last week. Our advance party had already left for Germany so they could get things sorted out for when the main party arrive. Then the day came it was GOES HOMMY DAY and we were off to the airport to get the GOES HOMMY BIRD.

I felt a real sense of achievement on leaving Northern Ireland I had done my job to the best of my ability, and had not let down any of my comrades' while I was out on the ground, be it in trucks or on patrol. I had gained a large amount of experience and respect from the other lads in the Sqn.

CHAPTER SEVENTEEN

With the first of my Northern Ireland tours completed and there were a few more to come, it was back to normal daily work. But that's what happens one minute you're away doing your bit for queen and country, and the next minute you're on your back scrubbing under a 10 tonne truck soaking in Kerosene.

Within the RCT you were moved around i.e. posted every three years to a different Squadron or to a Regt. You would be allowed to put your three preferences down to where you would like to go (Wish List). So it was always the plum postings you asked for, and tried to steer clear of the ones that were like penile Regts. If you were lucky and there was a place for you in one of these plum postings then you got it, but it was the decision of Manning and Records to where you went. Manning and Records were the Ivory Towers of the RCT, these people posted you, and told you how long you would be in that post for and they were also responsible for your Promotion.

Every year a confidential report would be written about you, it would contain everything you had done and your attitude over the last year. This would be written by your Staff Sergeant and Troop Commander, then your Officer Commanding would have his say, and finally you would be given a Grade. Now if you got a goose egg (O) outstanding grade then you was chuffed to bits, because you needed an O to be in with a shout of maybe getting promoted anything less than that and the Ivory Towers would not even look at it. There was over 10,000 personnel serving in the RCT when I joined all of different rank but the main bulk of the personnel where Drivers. There must have been about 7,000 of us, so you can imagine the competition was very high to try and get onto the first rung of the promotion ladder.

If you kept your nose clean and were good at your job, promotion would normally find you every three to four years, and of course your face had to fit. I was fortunate to get onto the promotion ladder in 1979 just after the NI tour. I say fortunate because I still think it is a lottery to get that First Tape onto your arm. There is a saying (The First Tape is the hardest to get and the easiest to loose) as I found out rather quickly. I was so happy and kept looking at my arm to make sure the tape was still there, and I had got it within my first three years.

After a couple of months you just got used to it and the extra pay was great, plus you also had the extra responsibility that came with it. They say shit rolls down hill and stops at the bottom well it always stopped with the

Lance Corporal i.e. my rank. It was down to us to bollock the drivers, and in some cases that was quite hard to do. Some of these drivers had served 8 years and there you were only having done three years and you're telling them the right from wrong, but I got through it somehow.

One particular evening there was about 7 of us down town where the locals made us more than welcome. We would visit the bars and nine times out of ten would end up getting drunk. We would then get a taxi to take us back to camp in the early hours of the morning. The taxi drivers would charge us double fare because we were normally too wasted to know the right price.

It was on this night that things got out of hand, the beer was flowing, the lights were flashing and on the record deck Bonny M was blaring out. An argument started between us and one of the natives and before we knew it a full fight was in progress, well you don't stand there and watch you get stuck in. The Police arrived and were trying to stop it. The natives stopped straight away, but not us we wanted to rule Germany and were not going to let a few policemen stop us. I remember hitting this Policeman and grabbing his neck and then I was being severely beaten by every copper in town, wow what a kicking.

I was arrested, photographed, and beaten up again for fun. I was driven back to camp where I thought that was it finished. The SSM was at the guardroom waiting for me and he was well pissed off, well it was about 0400hrs, and he knew everything that had happened. The SSM greeted me with a serenade of abuse that could be heard miles away, when he had finished and was pausing for breath I was thrown into a cell.

While trying my hardest to sober up and think of some wild excuse to account for my actions that evening I was brought back to reality when I heard the SSM shouting at anyone that was living he was not a happy chappy.

I was taken to my married quarter in the back of the land rover and was told to collect all my army kit ASAP. The time was about 0530hrs on a Sunday morning and the wife was sound asleep when I walk in and started to collect all my kit. A very quick explanation and don't worry I will see you in a few hours' time, and it was back into the vehicle and straight back to the cell. A sheet of paper was handed to me and I was told at 0800hrs there will be a cell inspection and your kit must be laid out like this and the door was slammed shut.

At 0800hrs the door was thrown open and in strolled the SSM, I was already standing to attention and said morning sir. Fucking morning it was when I was woken up by the OC telling me that his men were fighting with the police at about 3 this morning. He went straight to the bottom of the bed picked it up and turned it completely over and stood there looking at all my kit and bedding laying on the floor. He then moved slightly towards me, which made me move away from him, stand still Osborne don't you dare move. I thought here comes a beating but I was wrong it was just another serenade telling me what a wanker I was and how I was going to be reduced to the rank of driver on Monday morning, and to get my kit sorted out for another inspection at 1000hrs.

I sat on the bed and my brain was racing what can I do, what can I say, and each time the answer was nothing. I was going to lose my rank plus the little perks that went with it and of course the extra money, oh the wife is going to be so happy with me. I thought for a split moment how can they pre empt the verdict of my trail they cannot do that, I have rights I know the law. What a load of bollocks they can and will do what they want, they are the law.

At 0900hrs on Monday morning I was still a Lance Corporal in Her Majesty's Army, at 0910hrs I was back in my cell having received 7 days detention (jail) and reduced back to the rank of driver. I had two charges against me the first one was for striking a policeman, that's where I lost my rank, and the second charge was for being drunk and disorderly, and for that I got seven days in jail. Oh and by the way when you are in jail you do not get paid, oh the joys of getting drunk.

CHAPTER EIGHTEEN

My next posting in March 1980 was still in Germany which was handy and was only about 35 miles from where I was serving already so moving all our kit that we had amassed over the three years (which wasn't much) was quite easy. When you move into a married quarter it is already furnished with everything from a knife to a settee, but the stuff that is there for you to use is so out dated and horrible. Here are some examples the knife, fork, and spoons are about 12 inches long it's a skill trying to guide food into your mouth from that range. They give you a huge and I mean huge mincer this thing would not look out of place in a high street butchers. And the furniture was a multi coloured two seatter settee which was rock hard, and when you sat on it you was in a very up right military position. So what do you do you go out and buy your own stuff everything goes on tick and before you know it, there's more money going out then coming in but you try and manage.

The Squadron that I was posted to was a staff car sqn i.e. it had many cars some normal run a rounds, but they were mainly high class fancy motors for all the big wigs. This was completely different to what I had been doing for the last three years, but I was posted there and could not do anything about it. After a week or so I understood the role of the squadron and how it worked. It was a bit laid back, and not so military in the way of exercises and NI tours. Basically the sqns role was to transport officers from A to B in smart cars.

There was a lot of free time in the evenings and there was always something going on in the bar. So being a friendly sort of guy who likes a beer and a laugh I started to use the bar a lot, in fact I might as well have moved my bed in there it was like a magnet to me. The other thing about this sqn was that it had a lot of females serving in it. Can I just say at this point later on in my career I served in some pretty awful places, where you had to be good and strong, and take nothing away from those women in the forces, they do a great job and in some cases they are better than the guys I have never run them down and never will. I served in the 1st Gulf war with them, but that is another story which comes later, well done ladies.

So there I was working, drinking, partying, womanising, everything was great or so it seemed. My marriage was crumbling and my fitness was suffering, but the blinkers were on and I was having fun. Eventually my wife left me and took with her my two children and so I moved back into the block and became a single guy again. The male accommodation was right next door to the females' accommodation. I had started to sort my life out by laying of the booze and getting stuck into work. Of course I would go to the sqn bar and then onto the local bars but I did cut down on the drinking.

I had got my Lance corporal back and was getting good grades again, and new it would not be too long (if I kept my nose clean) before I would get my full Corporal (2 tapes).

I had started a relationship with this girl who was in the sqn and like all squaddies I fell head over heels for her to the extent that I was in her room more than mine. At night we would go out together have a laugh and then back to her room. Well someone dropped me in it and told the SSM that I was always in the female block and that I was sleeping there as well, something I denied flatly. One morning the SSM came into my room at 0700hrs and accused me of not sleeping in my bed as it was still made up. I explained to him that I had been out jogging at 0530hrs trying to keep up my fitness, this really pissed him of and I knew he was onto us. So now at night I would pull back the sheets mess up the bed and leave it so if he came in then there it was slept in.

One night I was in the girls room when a bang on the door startled us they banged again by this time I was out of the bed and peeped around the curtain only to find a military policeman standing at the window, shit how am I going to get out of this situation. The girl had answered there shouts of open the door by saying one minute just coming and crap like that, where could I go, behind the door was the only place how pathetic but there was nowhere else to go. So there I am bollock naked stood on tip toes, heels against the wall when she opened the door. Looking through the crack of the door I could see two female MPs, two male MPs and the SSM, wow what a search party all this for me.

They stood at the door and asked if she was alone to which she answered yes, can we come into your room and see for ourselves, and again she answered yes. Now my heart was out of my mouth banging away next to my balls on the floor what was she doing allowing them into her room. A deep breath and the door was pushed open to its max and in they came, they had a look around, and they even looked under the bed, and I could see them clearly, so they are bound to see me. The girl was stood by the door actually holding it open, when the SSM said ok and they all walked straight out. I could not believe my luck and that they never looked behind the door.

A little while after that incident I got promoted and was posted out of the Sqn in 1981 and back to where I had joined up in 1976 Aldershot, welcome home I thought but not everyone thought like me.

CHAPTER NINETEEN

First day at the new regt in Aldershot and I was as smart as a carrot. As I made my way down to the vehicle lines I kept looking at the 2 tapes on my arm, I was a full corporal. Get in there!. After the parade I was called into the sergeant majors office for a welcome to the Sqn chat or so I thought, not on your nelly. "Do you know why your here Corporal Osborne" was his first words, "posting on promotion sir I said with a slight grin", but the SSM thought differently. "Wrong Cpl Osborne, yes you were promoted and why I have no idea, but your here because you were kicked out of the Sqn for being a pain in the arse, and now I've ended up with you why Osborne why." I don't know why I answered standing looking straight at him thinking this is a great start to the next three years. You are here because nobody else wanted you, so fucking manning and records sent you to us. A pep talk then took place, which I might add was a one way conversation, I never spoke for about 5 minutes except at the end when I said ok Sir.
It was great to get back to a working unit there was lots of exercise, and we were supporting many units in the UK. The regt was all male and had about five hundred men. There was three Sqns in the regt so you can imagine there was a lot of rivalry between each Sqn. There was also a lot of rivalry between different cap badges especially when you were down town in the evening. We all thought we were better than the each other, and the civilians could never understand, why at the end of the evening we would kick the shit out of each other.
The girl I had been seeing in Germany was now serving in the UK, so we would meet up over the weekends. She would come down from the midlands by train on a Friday evening and stay in my bunk (own room) until Sunday. One particular weekend she was coming down by train and I said to my mate who by the way was a practical joker, that I was meeting the girl at the station and does he want to come down and have a couple of beers while waiting for the train. I was in the station toilets when the train arrived so when I came out I was surprised not to see the girl waiting there. My mate said he hadn't seen her and she may be on the next train. This went on all night until the last train came and went and she still had not turned up, oh well sod her I said to my mate let's get another beer. When I finally stumbled into my room and opened the door I shit myself, there she was in my bed asleep. Well what a bollocking I got, and trying to explain to a women who had just been woken up by some drunk, who was trying his

best to convince her that he was there at the station waiting for her. My mate had seen her get off the train and had told her I was up in the room waiting for her. I saw the funny side of it after a while but the girlfriend was not impressed.

The Regimental Sergeant Major was a strange man who had football eyes one at home and one away, and who smoked a pipe. We had a good relationship he hated me and I just loved winding him up. He had this white fluffy dog but the hair on his back was always singed. This would happen because he would bang his pipe on the edge of the table when in one of his rants, and the hot backi would fall onto the dog and singe his fur. You would be stood there getting a bollocking and there was this comedy act going on in front of you, the RSM trying to set fire to his dog.

The RSM had made me the President of the Mess Committee (PMC) of the corporals mess which basically meant, overseeing the daily running of the mess and the organisation of social events and functions. During the monthly mess meeting chaired by the RSM it was decided that a cheese and wine party would take place in the mess, and the dress code would be collar and tie for the men and cocktail dresses for the ladies, and the function was to be held on a Saturday evening.

The day before the function my mate (practical joker) and I had the day of work, this was so we could go down to the town and get all the wine and cheeses for Saturday evening. A grant of 800 Pounds had been voted over and I had it in my pocket ready to spend. At the checkout we stood with our three trolleys (each) full to the brim with a huge selection of different wines and feeling quite proud of our selections. The bill was about seven hundred and fifty pounds; well-done I thought at least we kept it inside the budget. The RSM will be so chuffed with us gold stars all round and a week of work ha ha. You got a lot of wine for that amount of money bearing in mind it was 1981, and with the last box loaded we were on our way.

We had not got very far when it dawned on me that we had not brought a single slice of cheese, and yet we had spent almost all the money on wine, that's it we are dead. With the wine unloaded and in the fridges it was time to get some more money for the cheese.

The RSM always went out for lunch which was a good thing, but the pay Sgt would always be in his office doing his books. So in I went and hatched this story/lie to him. I told him that I had spoken with the RSM and had informed him that there were more people coming to tomorrows night function then first expected, and he has authorised me to get another five hundred pounds so here I am. Well I just cannot give out that sort of money just like that, and also the RSM will need to sign for it. I represent the RSM don't I, with my position as the PMC and he is at lunch and I need to go shopping. With the five hundred pounds in my pocket we were back down town spending it all on cheese. There were cheeses I had never heard of, I had long ones, fat one, round ones, stinking ones, runny ones you name it I had it. The function went great and there was gallons of wine and tons of cheese left at the end of the night, so not to be wasteful I was handing it out to people when they left. People were leaving with a box of wine under there arm or a roll of cheese in the wife's bag, who cares take it home with you and enjoy.

My mate and I were summoned to the RSMs office first thing Monday morning and I knew something was not right, as his dog was already smoldering. He asked how the night went, great I answered everyone had a great time, good glad to hear it he said. He then told me he would get someone to take the cheese and wine that was left from the function over to the Sgts Mess. There is none I told him it's all gone, at this time the dog sensing that an explosion was imminent he moved away from the table he had been burnt enough. "Well how much wine is left then" he asked, that's all gone as well sir. How ?how? how ?I don't believe you Osborne, so I butted in and told him that I had given it all away.

By now the dog had left the room sensible move on his part because the RSM through his pipe at the wall which broke into many pieces and landed all over the carpet. He was now a stuttering wreck; he couldn't put two words together let alone a sentence. He kept on standing up but never went anywhere then he would sit back down, shaking his head quickly from side to side and was looking very red. There was nothing else that could infuriate him even more or was there. My mate said "excuse me Sir I need to tell you something," "what do you want to tell me" he yelled, "your carpet is smoldering sir". The RSM leapt out of his chair and walked over to the smoldering patches and started to stamp on them, only to realise that the carpet was nylon and was sticking to his shoes. When he lifted his shoe up there would be melted nylon stretching from his shoe to the carpet. We went to help him but were told not to move and stay where we were so we did. Then my world collapsed the Pay Sgt knocked on the door and asked the RSM to counter sign for the extra five hundred pounds which he was told he had authorised.

Myself and my mate where given 30 extra duties each this meant every other day we would be on guard duty. So during the working week it was work as normal and then get ready for guard mount at 1800 hrs. The following morning we would report to the RSM to say all is well and then go to work absolutely knackered. When it was the weekend you was on duty for twenty four hours at a time. Getting extra duties was a way of getting punished and not having to go in front of the old man and getting charged, it was a choice you was given, do extras or get charged.

It was while carrying out one of my extra duties that I fell fowl of the RSM again. It was a Sunday afternoon and the Salvation Army tea vehicle had turned up at the guardroom ringing its bell. I explained to the lady that she was not welcome here and she had to leave. God! she moaned and moaned in the end I said go and take your God squad tea wagon somewhere else. A few moments later the phone rang, it was the RSM having a major fit down the phone. I told him yes sir that's right some old women from the sally army trying to sell tea and buns, so I fucked her off you know sir security got to keep on the ball. Yes sir, yes sir, I see sir, ok sir I will see you Monday morning and put the phone down. Everyone in the guardroom was looking at me and saying what's wrong, I told them that the old lady we had told to go away and sell her tea somewhere else was in fact the RSMs wife. I got five more extra duties on top of what I had already been given, but it was all worth it in the end. The cheese and wine party was talked about for years; it went down in the Regts history and is still talked about today by those who were there at the time.

CHAPTER TWENTY

My three years spent in Aldershot had its ups and downs and of course it's good and bad times, but the good times outweighed the bad times easily. Yes I had the odd run in with the RSM and the Squadron Sgt Majors maybe a few to many but I was young and cocky and always spoke my mind, which was not the thing to do in the early 80s. It was still very much the old school back then, you done what you were told with no questions asked. Later on during my service it proved to be an asset to be able to speak up against certain things that were being done, rather than just sitting there being a yes man.
The Regiment supported many other units in Aldershot, like the Infantry for instance and when they went on exercise a Sqn from the Regt would be detailed to give them logistic support. This sounded great you would just pick them up and take them from A to B and let them play soldiers, and then you would bring them back, drop them off and park up and go to sleep. How wrong was I in fact when a Sqn was attached to a unit for their exercise you became one of them for the whole duration, the driving part was a part time job.
One of these exercises was going to take place in Germany and the Sqn I was in got the job of supporting them. It was a four weeks exercise and was taking place in Hamburg in West Germany (as it was known then). I was on my way back to Germany for four weeks, beer, bratties (German sausage) but most important of all I was away from the camp. No RSM yelling at you just because you're alive and breathing; no room or block jobs, no guardroom duties, nothing just four weeks of bliss bring it on.
The exercise was going great and everyone had done well, there was no major cock ups, no embarrassing moments for the boss, nobody was injured, and best of all the unit we were supporting where impressed with our professionalism and attitude. Well that was until we were given some R & R.
There was to be a four day break during the exercise for everyone. This is a time to basically chill out, get some washing done, catch up on some sleep, go down town have a couple of beers, see the sites, and behave yourselves. Well after a couple of days I had done all my admin i.e. washing, catching up on sleep, and it was my turn to go down town. So it was on with the Jeans, a good fitting T shirt, your desert willies, all squaddies had a pair of these light brown swede ankle boots, they looked the dogs bollocks with

jeans and a wallet full of Deutch marks. We got dropped off at a designated point and were told that the tpt would be here at certain times to take us back to camp. We were free, to go out and enjoy ourselves have a couple of beers and take in the sights.

My mate and I broke away from the rest of the crowd and headed straight for the red light district and started checking out the bars. A quick beer here, a beer there, a lot of window shopping was done but we didn't buy anything. After a few hours of pacing ourselves two or three beers an hour we were now getting into the swing of things in Hamburg. We met up with some Americans and that was it the challenging started. Who could do the most press ups and pull ups, who had the most tattoos, who could drink the fastest beer, so on, so on. At one point there were about 8 of us stood in this bar in just our underpants getting ready to do the dance of the flaming arseholes. What you do is roll some toilet paper up insert it into ones back side and someone lights it. You then dance on a table with this paper on fire hanging out of your arse, and the winner is the one who lets it burn the longest. Myself and my mate came out champions even though we had some slight burns on our bum cheeks, the yanks thought we were mad and should be locked up.

By the time we left the bar we had lost all track of time but we didn't care, more window shopping, more beers, and of course some food. The beer was now taking its toll on us and also the money was running out fast. There was one bar we went in and they charged us sixty four Marks for two beers. There was no point in arguing as there was bouncers everywhere and we were in know fit state to stand let alone fight, so we paid up and left.

There we were in the early hours of the morning swaying around and not making much sense when we spoke to each other. We were trying to work out how to get back to camp as we had missed the transport and only had a couple of hours to get back before all hell was let loose. We decided to get a train back to the town where we were staying but had little money left so we were allowed to get onto the carriage that had the mail and newspapers on it. Great we were on our way, we both said we shall stay awake so we would not miss our stop but we both fell asleep. We had also got onto the wrong train and it was heading south. We woke up and climbed out of the carriage trying to work out where we were, about a seven hour drive away from the rest of the Sqn that's where we were, oh shit try and get out of this one Ossie. After a free train ride back to where we were meant to be we arrived back at camp to a wonderful reception.

The two of us were charged and given a three months warning order each, another words step out of line again within the next three months and you will lose your rank. The rest of the exercise went well and I kept my head down and out of trouble.

CHAPTER TWENTY-ONE

I had just passed my HGV Class1 and also my motor bike test and was just about to start my SMQC (senior military qualification course) this was one of the courses you needed if you wanted to be considered for the rank of Sergeant. Having passed the SMQC course my Sqn was off to Cyprus for an exercise. The exercise was to be run as an inter squadron exercise where each troop had three sections and would compete against each other in everything from fitness, to shooting, first aid, survival skills, combat skills, and much much more. It was extremely hard going but at the end of the exercise my section had come out on top we had won. So now I was the golden boy, I couldn't do anything wrong or could I, of course I could.

The SSM and the OC had agreed with the local Cypriot police to send about thirty personnel down to their training compound and help out with their riot control training phase. Myself and another CPL who was a Physical Training Instructor were in charge of this little bonding exercise between our two countries what could go wrong.

The police were there in there riot gear, shields, and batons drawn, we were in jeans and trainers. After a quick brief from there commander we went outside and started to form a rowdy crowd, and moved towards the police lines. We started to push against their shields, when a couple of the police started getting a bit heavy handed with their batons. A few of the lads started getting hit around the legs and arms quite hard; one had been hit in the mouth and was bleeding. This was not in the script so myself and the other Cpl decided a cunning plan was in order. I told the lads the next time we go forward we go in as one and hit them hard, and everyone is to get stuck in.

We ran at them and got straight through the shields and started to get about the police what a hectic five or so minutes, there was injuries everywhere it had turned into a proper fight. We left with our heads held high, that will teach them to fuck around with the British Squaddie. When we returned to camp I was summoned straight away to the SSM s office. I could not get a word in anywhere, I tried to explain what had happened but it fell on deaf ears. The police had phoned the SSM and had told him that I had instigated a real riot and that his men had done nothing wrong. Back in front of the OC again and again I got a three months warning order. All that good hard work that I had done over last few months had gone out of the window; I was a trouble maker again what a load of crap.

A couple of us were detailed to cover the beach guard which had to be done every night, and was the easiest guard you would ever do while in the Army. You were to stay on the beach during the night and look after the canoes. With a little shack on the beach open until late selling food and beer this was a great duty. I went for a swim at about 2300 hrs. and was floating around when my mate was shouting Ossie Ossie get in get in there is a shark behind you. Well you hear it all the time yeah yeah ok I will play along with you. Help help shark shark and I started to splash about and bob up and down. My mate was waving his arms like there was no tomorrow and was screaming get out Ossie there is a shark out there. So I turned around and there it was about 100 mtrs away, I saw the fin sticking out of the water and shit myself. It was not facing me or coming towards me but it was there. I headed straight for the beach which was only about twenty to thirty metres away but it seemed like miles. My arms were racing through the water, and my feet were pounding away like pistons. I do not remember breathing, as I made my way to safety but I did swallow about a pint of sea water, and all the time I was waiting for the bite. I finally swam up the beach and was shaking like a leaf; it took me ages to get my breath back. But once I had I sat there looking out at the ocean and saw the fin a couple of more times. In the morning I asked the shack owner do you get sharks around here at night or even during the day and he said with a smile OF COURSE.

Another funny thing happened to a friend of mine who I still keep in contact with, while out swimming he saw and grabbed an Octopus. It was a fair size and as it was trying its hardest to get away so he cradled it against his stomach, seconds later he let out an almighty scream. He was trying to pull the octopus off of him, but the octopus had his beak well and truly sunk into his side. Everyone was in bits and in typical Squaddie humour nobody went to help him we were all rolling around with laughter, my friend survived and so did the octopus, well it survived to bite another day.

I had managed to keep out of trouble for well over a year I don't know how, perhaps lady luck was on my side and I just never got caught, It was that or the system had just given up on me who knows. I now had a new posting order and I was to report to Berlin on the 2nd of January 1984. I had recently got married to a girl who I had met at Stonehenge, yes you read it right, Stonehenge, I had gone there for the week and what a week it was. We had just got back from the Falklands and were given three weeks leave so I packed a bag with a few items and off I went with my mate and drove to Stonehenge.

Hanging out with stoned hippies was an eye opener I'm pretty sure they did not even know they were there. We were there for the music which was brilliant and the booze which was not that brilliant. We brought something that resembled scrumpy that was sold in a 5 litre container, it was a bit hazy and the liquid was still fermenting but it was cheap so we got some. It done the job, I had a massive hangover and I felt like shit that day but then went and got some more. There is a picture of me somewhere dancing with a policeman in the middle of the stones just as the sun was coming up; it's amazing what that so called scrumpy does to your brain.

CHAPTER TWENTY-TWO

Christmas 1983 was a bit hectic I had a lot of things to get done before I could leave Aldershot. All my bedding had to be handed in, and you had to visit all the department heads in the regiment where they would sign your clearance chit after checking you do not have anything on signature from there department. Once that is all done you go in front of the SSM and then in front of the OC who wishes you farewell and good luck. When that is all over you get your travel documents, and as I was driving to Berlin there was a lot of paper work to get sorted out. With all the Ts crossed and the eyes dotted I was on my way driving through France, Belgium, and Germany and also along the Berlin Corridor. I arrived at my new Sqn on time be it a little tired but I was there, good morning Berlin.
The role of my new Sqn was a little bit different to what I had just been doing for the last three years. We had civilians working with us, and our main role was to support the staff of the Brigade. If they wanted a car then they got a car, If a coach was required to go over to the eastern part of Berlin then we provided it. This was going to be a very cushtie two years of my Army Career as long as I kept my nose clean.
The vehicles were in immaculate condition there was not a scratch or a speck of dust to be seen. A lot of these vehicles were used for ceremonial parades i.e. Allied forces parade and of course the Queen's Birthday parade so they were kept in a pristine condition. It was a very relaxed atmosphere at work and as long as all the details got done during the day then there was no need to shout and ball at people.
After a couple of months I decided to take up boxing, it seemed a good thing to volunteer for at the time, no duties, no guards, just training. My fitness was quite high but as soon as I started doing the boxing training I realised this was not going to be a walk in the park. My trainer was a Sgt in the Sqn and he ran me ragged both day and night, he had just 2 months to get me ready for my 1st ever fight in a ring. He would be sitting in his Porsche driving along beside me, barking out orders like (sprint to the next post, now jog to that post, Give me 20 sit-ups, and so on) and all the time he is sat in his car listening to Stevie Wonder. The training was hard but very good and I had lost any fat that I had, I had also bulked up quite a bit and was dead on my fighting weight which was Light Heavy.
The Berlin Boxing Championships had arrived and it was taking place in the Cupersol arena. It was to be a inter unit competition, another words it

was open to all British units serving in Berlin at that time. I arrived at the arena with my trainer and when I looked inside I was amazed at the size of the arena it was huge, and in the middle of all those seats was a large ring just waiting for you to enter it. Well I found out who I was going to fight by looking at this huge board and the time that I was fighting. I watched a couple of fights but they were over very quickly and I wondered if my fight would be over that fast. My time had arrived and out I went I wasn't nervous I just wanted to get in there and get it done. My trainer was telling me to do this and make sure I done that and before I knew it the bell went. A few blows were thrown and down he went and he never made the count, I had won my first fight. My trainer was chuffed to bits and I had not even broke sweat this boxing game is a doddle. My next fight was coming up and as I was getting ready my opponent's trainer came in and said his boy had hurt his wrist and was pulling out of the fight. I had won again and now I was through to the last eight. These fights were to take place in the evening that was when the public could come in and watch.

For the rest of the day I tried to relax but was getting more nervous as the time ticked by, and the place was filling up with people. The time had arrived and I was ready to go again, as I walked out into the arena I could hear people cheering and shouting out my name (go on Ossie knock him out) it seemed the whole Squadron was there shouting for me. As I climbed into the ring everything around me went quite, all I could hear was my trainer talking to me, it's amazing how that happens I couldn't even hear any of the crowd. The bell went and we were off, a couple of jabs here and there and then WACK he smacked me straight in the middle of my face wow that stung, and I wondered if my brain was still in my head, and do I still have a nose on my face. End of the round and back to the corner to get wiped down and to rinse my mouth out. I must have drunk half the water in the bottle and when the bucket was offered for me to spit out the water, I just looked at him and smiled.

The bell went for the second round and it was back out again and getting beaten up. Then all of a sudden I had connected with him, a right hand had smacked him square in the face and he went back against the ropes. His legs had gone, but for some reason I never went into him and finished him off I just stood back and let him get his head back together. Round 3 was a slugging match toe to toe throughout the whole round and then the bell went. I had lost the fight on a split decision but I had done it, I never went down and I had gone the three rounds, I knew I could do it, so always believe in yourself. Monday morning and I was back at work still sore, with both eyes still swollen I was a bit of a hero even though I had lost.

CHAPTER TWENTY-THREE

Rudolf Hess was still being housed in Spandau Prison in 1984 and every now and then it came down to the squadron to provide the guard for this facility. We would be there for a week locked in the prison with the most famous prisoner in the world basically doing two hours on duty and four hours off duty for a week. I only got picked to do this once and that was enough, after the week you was absolutely ball bagged. Everything was so strict you had to march out to the towers and you were not allowed to look around, and if Hess caught you looking at him, he would report you to your superiors and you were then in the shit. I did manage to see him once when he was in his garden tottering around just looked like a normal old man.
The British, Americans, and the Soviets, would take turns in guarding Hess for a month at a time, and the rumour on the street was (do not know how true this is) that whoever was guarding Hess at the time he died they would be able to stay in the prison. This was concerning for the Brits and the Yanks, as they did not want the Soviets in West Berlin.
There was a British Army barracks next door to the prison and I remember seeing on a number of occasions their tanks had been turned around and parked facing towards Spandau Prison whenever the Soviets where guarding him. Would they have destroyed the prison if the soviets were guarding Hess at the time when he died who knows but that was the rumour on the streets?
Doing the guard at Spandau Prison was an experience but once was enough the prisoner was treated better than us. Another duty we got involved in was guarding the Berlin train as it went through East Berlin and through to Dresden this was another pain in the arse duty. You would start at 0600hrs in the morning and finish about 2000hrs that night and all you done was sit on the train. You were not allowed off the train, the train never carried any passengers, the doors were locked, the only good thing about it was you saw real Russian Soldiers, and you got good food. It was a complete waste of time and money. I done a few of these guards during my time in Berlin, and if I was comparing it to the other duties I had done in the army this one was a cushy number.

The eighteen months I spent in Berlin were great ,I had learnt a lot about the history and saw the historic Berlin wall that had been erected around the city. Check point Charlie was a great place to visit along with the museum as well as the trips over to the Eastern part of Berlin. You had a lot of spare time on your hands and this was not a good thing for me. There was a watering hole (pub) right outside the camp gates. You would pop in for a beer after work with all the good intensions of leaving and going home after you finished it, but that never happened. A beer would lead to two, then five, then ten until you were drunk and happy and of course you now wanted to go down town. Many times we would end up in the town still in uniform chatting to the locals, and finally getting home at three o'clockish in the morning. And of course you would have ordered your very large hangover the day before, and there it was, waiting for you in the morning.

One particular evening I was in the watering hole and having a good time with the lads when the door opened and in walked the wives all dressed up and ready to go out for the evening down the town. They were going to have a quick drink with us and then they would be of to paint the town red. It was now the early hours in the morning and they were still there having a great time singing, dancing and making fools of themselves, just like us men do when we are drunk. The next day I am glad to say was a Saturday, and yes the big hangover had arrived first thing in the morning and on time for both of us.

Road works were happening outside the local pub and had been there for about three weeks, but this particular night I must have forgotten all about them. As I woke up I realised I was not in my bed, in fact I was not in any bed, and I could hear the noise of traffic close by. I was laying there looking up at the sky and watching the clouds when I felt the rain landing on my face, but on both sides of me all I could see was earth. Was I laying in an open grave, had I died that night, couldn't my wife afford to put me in a box, come on what's happening.

I got to my feet and as I stood up my chest was level with the road, and I'm looking at cars passing by within a foot of my head. Still in uniform I managed to climb out of the hole and get my arse back home and got changed. When I had left the pub I must have forgotten all about the road works, and fell straight into the hole and had slept there overnight, what a state to get into!!.

CHAPTER TWENTY-FOUR

There is the one big event that dwarfs everything in Berlin and that is the Queen's Birthday Parade. The train guard, guarding Hess, and the other parades, they are important of course but compared to this parade they were nothing. They don't come any bigger than this parade and this has to run absolutely perfect, there are no room for errors.
Preparation starts weeks before the event and there is no let up at all. Every unit serving in Berlin will take part in this parade and the parade is completely performed with the use of military vehicles being driven around inside a very large stadium. The vehicles that we would supply for the parade were land rovers, and large trucks, and they were to be immaculate. They are painted and then painted again until they look brand new; every part of the vehicle gets painted even the tires.
We had spare vehicles which we would use to practice all the driving maneuvers that we would have to complete during the parade. Day in day out practice practice until we got it perfect. With a week to go everything was in order the vehicles were ready; we all knew the maneuver's that had to be done, and our uniforms were gleaming. Then came the day before the big parade, it started of great all the vehicles were driven down to the stadium and parked up in its designated place, wiped down and left with the keys inside. There was also a huge guard force in operation that day and night. Once all the vehicles were parked up in the stadium all those taking part in the parade were stood down for the rest of the day.
So after all the intense preparation we were finally ready, so a few of us decided to go and have a beer at the local pub outside the camp. After a couple of beers I was about to head of home when a couple of mates came in, so not wanting to be rude I had a couple with them, and before I knew it I was on the slippery slope, day turned into night and my nightmare had just started.
Morning had arrived and yours truly had not noticed it because I was still sound asleep in my scratcher. The door was being kicked off its hinges and loud voices were shouting out Ossie get up, get up. I leapt out of bed and opened the door and was in shock, I was looking at five guys in parade uniform and they were just staring at me in my underpants. Fuck me this cannot be happening this has to be a dream, surely I haven't slept in, and especially not on her Majesty's Birthday Parade, but I had and I had about ten minutes to get my arse in gear. Supporting a massive hangover I told

the guys give me ten minutes and I will be there just wait in the mini bus. I was running around in circles trying to have a shave, and trying to get dressed was a major ordeal. Somehow and even to this day I still do not know how I achieved it, but I did and now I was in the mini bus and on my way to the stadium.

Hot and sweaty and feeling sick I just sat there like Billy no mates. I knew I had let the guys down this morning, but we were not on parade and I would not let them down once we get out there. Opening the side door of the bus I threw my head out and chucked up at a set of traffic lights. The people waiting to cross the road were not expecting this first thing in the morning, but they got it a pavement pizza everywhere.

Feeling a lot better we arrived at the stadium and went over to our vehicles and waited for the parade to start. The vehicle I was in was an open top Land Rover and I was to stand in the passenger's foot well while we drove around the stadium. The vehicles would be driven around four a breast, and when we came along the straight towards the saluting dais, I would tap the top of the window screen. This being the signal to the other guys in there land rovers to get ready to carry out the salute.

Feeling very ill again and after more paracetamol the parade started, and after about 20 minutes it was time for the drive past. The vehicles all started together and pulled away at the same time perfect, but not all was perfect inside my stomach. My driver asked me a number of times if I was ok and if I wanted to stop.

All I had to do was put my arm in the air and that would show to the others that we had broken down. No way not a chance don't you dare stop I will be ok keep going mate. The saluting dais was filled with Royalty, and Senior Military Staff, and there were thousands of people watching the parade from the stands. We had about fifty metres to go before I had to give the signal for the salute, when my stomach decided it wanted out again. I tried my hardest to keep it down but there is only so much one can swallow before it has to come out, and that is exactly what happened. In fact I was quite impressed with the timing, I turned my head to the right and with one almighty reach from the stomach it was out. As if part of a drill movement I turned my head to the front and gave the signal for the salute, which was carried out with accurate and precise timing. We drove past the dais and back to the positions where we had started from, and watched the rest of the parade. My driver could not believe I had made it through the parade and to be honest neither could I.

Did anybody see me throw up I don't think so; they are always too busy looking at the big picture so I thought I had got away with it. Not on your nelly there is always someone who will notice something out of the ordinary, and my troop Staff Sergeant had spotted me being sick. When we got back to camp I got a major bollocking and was charged, with being late for the transport in the morning, and being drunk on parade. I couldn't argue against the charges and was fined one week's pay, ouch that hurt. Even though it had cost me a week's pay, I felt a deep feeling of satisfaction inside, I had proved to myself yet again that I had the strength and balls to get on with the job, when seemingly everything was against me

CHAPTER TWENTY-FIVE

I It's June 1985 and I am on the move again this time to a regiment in Germany which has the reputation of being a penal regiment within the RCT. Everybody tried there hardest to avoid this posting and if you were unlucky enough to get posted there, then there was a good reason for it. Every year in every RCT unit throughout the world an officer is dispatched from Manning and Records (Ivory Towers) and visits that regiment or squadron. The purpose of these visits is for individual soldiers to be able to have a one on one with the officer and to discuss his or her career and where is it going.

One of these visits was taking place in Berlin just days before I was getting posted, so I took the opportunity and requested a personal interview to find out where my career was going.

Downhill at a great speed of knots that was his answer as simple as that. He basically told me that I could achieve a good rank, and that I was more than capable of achieving this. He looked back over my reports and said you keep letting yourself down in one way or another. I knew exactly what he was getting at; he did not have to tell me, it was staring me in the face. And the reason why Manning and Records had posted me to this Regt was to give me one more chance to get my life sorted out. This was the place where if you were good at your job, then it would be recognised by all, and maybe you could get your career back on course. But this regiment was also known to have destroyed many a career. So there it was in a nut shell go there and carry on the way you have been doing and expect to stay at the rank of corporal, which by the way is a great rank to hold, or knuckle down and get your career back on course.

I sometimes would question an order I was given, like why are we doing it that way when this way is quicker and it would take less time. The types of orders that I questioned were not life threatening, we were not at war, it's just that I could see other ways of doing things. This had been noticed by certain people in the past and remarks had previously been made on my yearly report. Comments like, he has the ability to lead and command at a high level, and has the respect of his subordinates. He relishes new challenges and will always give 100 % commitment to whatever tasks he is given. From the day I Joined the army I always looked at those with rank and said to myself I could do their job, and one day I would be doing their job, well that's what I thought.

As I got up to leave the room after my interview the officer said to me, Cpl

Osborne you have a very good career in front of you, do not waste it. I saluted and left the room feeling a bit deflated, but also looking forward to getting to my new posting and start proving to people that I have what it takes to be a good leader and an excellent team member. It was not going to be easy but I had always believed in my ability's, and I was not about to change my beliefs.

CHAPTER TWENTY-SIX

I had reported to my new Squadron and had completed all the documentation that goes with arriving at a new post. The regiment was huge, there were 4 squadrons that made up the Regt and there was a fierce rivalry between each of them. I was back in the army again, after spending eighteen months in a cushy military type of unit this was going to be a culture shock. The regiments roll was massive supporting all the units in the northern part of Germany. Exercises to Canada (Batus) were a regular feature for one of the Sqns during the year. Northern Ireland was also a regular commitment for one of the four Sqns a 4 month tour was always around the corner. Supporting other units in the field be it a week or three weeks, there was always some exercise going on. Finally on top of this you had your normal training to do within the regt, so there was not much time off.

I had already moved into my new married accommodation and the furniture had arrived from Berlin so I was ready to go. A lot of my neighbours where people I had already served with and this made it a lot easier to settle in.

There was a perimeter fence that encircled the whole camp, and on top of the fence was rolls of barbed wire, apparently it was there to keep us in, and no wonder this regt had a reputation of being a bastard of a place to get posted too.

The calendar was fairly full and the Sqn was in for a busy last six months of the year, this did not bother me, in fact I was looking forward to throwing myself 100 % back into military life. After a week I was back in the right frame of mind, Berlin was history, it was good fun but that was all it was. It did not take long to realise that this regt was a very professional unit; you are surrounded by people who are very good at their jobs. There were soldiers who had completed five or six tours of Northern Ireland, soldiers who had been attached to Infantry units like the Para's or the Marines. This regt had got a bad reputation for one reason and one reason only. If you were a wanker, a waster, or a shirker, your life would be made hell. The regts unwritten policy was you would not get an early posting; if you're posting order said 3 years, then it was 3 years simple as that.

There was always someone within a unit who would think they could beat the system. There was this lad who tried his hardest to convince everyone that he was depressed and needed to get out of the regt. This went on for at least a month and even the medical officer had dismissed his pleas of being depressed. I was in the SSMs office one day and we were having a conversation about something, when the so called depressed lad was knocking on his door. He had the sleeves of his jumper pulled up to his elbows and you could clearly see that the lad had cut his wrists and was leaking blood. The Sergeant Major sat up in his chair and told the soldier "If you drop any of your blood on my carpet I will charge you, do you understand young man". The soldier lifted his arms up in the air so any blood would run down his arms, and not onto the carpet. The SSM then called for the chief clerk to get this piece of shit out of his office and down to the med Centre. The soldier was charged with self-harming himself with a knife and this cost him a week's pay. He was to stay in the regt right up until his posting date was due.

I had my own section of vehicles and my own section of lads who were a great bunch of guys. I got there respect straight away as I would never asked them to do anything that I could not do myself. If we needed to work late then we all stayed late if a guy wanted to get away early for some reason, then we would all cover for him, and nobody would be any the wiser. The weeks and months rolled by and I loved it. I had got a few exercises under my belt and had proved to those senior to me that I knew my job when it came to working in the field, and my man management skills were pretty good as well. I had not been in any trouble, or upset anyone, and I was really happy here and they say a happy bunny is a good bunny.

Christmas and New Year had come and gone without any incidents and we were all back at work. We had a busy year ahead of us including an exercise in Canada which would last eight weeks; this was to take place during the months of May and June. It was a particular cold winter in the early months of 1986 and we making preparations to go on exercise in February. My enthusiasm was a little bit low for this exercise, I mean who wants to live in a hole in the woods in the middle of February with temperatures dipping below zero not me, but we were all in the same boat, so it was a case of just get on with it.

I was even asked to get involved with some of the planning which had to be done; normally this is sorted out at OC, SSM, and Senior NCO level. So being asked for my input and to get involved in the exercise conferences, was a great boost to my confidence and great for my self-esteem. My points and ideas were listened to; some were taken on board and the others ones were thrown out. I hated it when an idea of mine was thrown out, and when that happened I felt I had let myself down and also those around me, but this was a learning curve. When any of my ideas were thrown out I would ask WHY is that a bad idea and would not let go until one or two things happened. I got a decent explanation as to why my idea was not worthy, or the sergeant major would say Osborne shut the fuck up, which of course I did.

The exercise involved a lot of infantry tactics which in a way was good for my section, as we would learn from those who do this type of work day in day out, and as we were detached from the rest of the squadron it was a case of getting stuck in and hopefully learn from it. The unit we were supporting treated us like we were one of their own, no different. We were basically the enemy and we would attack them during the day and night. I would be given a grid reference to be at for a certain time, where we would set up a defence position, and await further orders. We would move tactically never knowing if we would get attacked ourselves, and on arriving at our new position we would then dig in.

Tonight's orders were to get inside the enemy's defence and leave pieces of card tapped to certain things with bomb written on them and get out without being noticed. We had all night to do this and it was up to me when and how we carried this out. I sat and wrote my orders and then briefed the lads on how we were going to execute this. There OC was there when I gave the briefing which I thought was strange but I got on with it.

Next morning as we sat in our position watching and smiling, you could hear shouting coming from the enemies direction this was because there were cards with bomb written on them all over there location. We had got in there and got out without being noticed and there OC was not a happy man.

The end of the exercise came and we said our goodbyes and set of back to camp with our heads held very high. The next day I was called into the OCs office and congratulated for doing a very good job, and that there OC was very impressed as well. With my head a little bigger I left the room and went back to work. I passed the well done onto all the guys and as expected they went and mouthed of to the other lads in the Sqn at how good they were. Inter Squadron rivalry is great; it gets the best out of people.

CHAPTER TWENTY-SEVEN

 The SSM wanted to see me ASAP what for I did not know but I jogged up to his office and tapped on his door, "you want to see me Sir" "Not just me Osborne but also the RSM what have you been up to", Nothing Sir. My mind was racing and I was trying to think what had I done, but nothing was coming to mind, but the SSM was having a fit. Get yourself down to the RSMs office now because you have fucked up big time. I stood outside the RSMs office with a heartbeat of at least 160 beats per minute, and a brain that could not work out what I had done.
The RSM came out of his office just looked at me and walked straight into the Colonels office and slammed the door. Bloody hell I must really be in the shit. Seconds later it opened and I was ordered into the office and the door closed behind me.
I was stood to attention still trying to think what I had done wrong when the Commanding Officer said "have you any idea why you are here Cpl Osborne", no Sir. He then stood up and said "I have an order here from Manning and Records saying, that you are to be promoted to the substantive Rank of Sergeant with immediate effect". My head was completely blown away me a sergeant, I could not believe it, I shook the COs hand, and said something like thank you sir and left his office. The RSM took me into his office and congratulated me, but he also told me how many things will change now that I was a Senior NCO. My squadron Sergeant Major congratulated me as well as the OC. The OC also told me that I would be staying in the Sqn and would be taking over from my Admin Sgt who was moving on to pastures new.
The next few days were a blur as I was trying to get my kit sorted out; I needed to get my new rank sown onto my shirts, jumpers, and parade dress uniform. I also had to buy a mess dress uniform for the formal nights that I would now be attending in the Sgts Mess. The wife would have had to get a long dress and also a couple of cocktail dresses. All this extra cost did not come cheap and it made a bit of a dent in our money.
The pay difference between a Cpl and a Sgt was about 3 pounds a day which was not to be sniffed at, but then you would get a mess bill every month. This bill would include anything that you have had during that month while in the mess. Example if you had tea and toast at Ten o'clock then that would cost you 50p a day. If you popped in for your dinner that would cost you as well, so at the end of the month your Mess bill would be

about thirty five to Forty pounds. So you're not really that much better off but that did not worry me at all I had made it to the Rank of Sergeant.

The sergeants mess is the most exclusive mess, club, call it what you want in the world. You cannot buy your way into it you have to earn the right to be in it. The officer's mess is completely different, once the officer has passed his training he is in the officers mess. It takes about seven to nine years or maybe longer to get into the Sgts Mess but once you get there it's a different life compared to the naaffi and I was about to find out.

You are treated completely different, the SSMs will actually talk to you, instead of giving you bollockings, and the officers have more respect for you as they know how long it has taken you to get that rank. Even though I had made the rank of sergeant I still hung around with my mates and partied with them when we were away from work. At work I was the Sgt, out of work I was Ossie the guy that they all knew. This did not go down to well with some people. On a few occasions I was reminded that I was a Senior NCO and that I should not be seen out and about with Junior Ranks. Senior NCOs should be seen with their own kind and if they want a drink then you go to the mess and drink. Not a chance I had known some of these guys my entire army career and they were good friends, and if it didn't go down to well with some people, then it was there problem, I was not going to change

CHAPTER TWENTY-EIGHT

. Sitting at Brize Norton and waiting for our flight to Canada was getting a drag, the guys were getting restless, and that could lead to trouble. The troop that was going to Canada was made up with a young Lieutenant who was the troop commander, a troop staff sergeant, the admin sgt who was me, and finally about 50 men of different rank. Football was the only answer and if by magic a football appeared, and before you knew it goals were set up using kit bags, the lines for the pitch was chalked onto the floor and the match had started. The match had been going for about ten minutes when some high ranking RAF officer appeared and was not impressed with what he saw. With the bollockings taken, and the football put away, we finally got onto the plane and we were on our way, Canada here we come.

Here we were in Canada, and getting ready for the live firing exercise, which would take place over the next few weeks. We had about a week to collect and sign for all the vehicles and equipment that we would need so we could play our part in this large exercise. Finally the battle group were ready to go; we had had so many briefings we were briefed out. It was drummed into every one of us to remember that this is a LIVE FIRING EXERCISE.

The exercise would be controlled by umpires who live with you day and night, they are also constantly in contact with each other. Tanks would be firing live shells, the mortars that would be fired are for real, and the rounds that we would be firing from our weapons would also be very real.

Night time out on the prairie is cold and pitch black, and not a place to go wondering around by yourself. We had received orders telling us to move to another position under the cover of darkness, so we packed up everything and moved out. No lights were to be used, it was to be a total black out and we had about five miles to travel to our new location. At one point the non-drivers had to walk about ten feet in front of the vehicles to make sure they did not go into the ditches that were on both sides of the track.

As we crept along the track it started to rain and this was making it very slippery for people to walk on. All of a sudden there were three almighty explosions which were pretty close by and this was followed by gun fire, we were in an ambush. The umpire was shouting out "no vehicles had been hit drive through it, no vehicles had been hit". The guys that were walking in front of the vehicles had picked themselves up and climbed into the trucks. With no vehicles being hit and apparently no casualties according to the umpire, we floored the accelerator and got out of the killing zone. We were clear of the ambush according to the umpire, so we pulled up and set up a quick guard and went and checked that we had everyone.

One truck missing and three men, who had forgot to pick up their co driver during the attack. A quick check of who was with whom soon identified who was missing. I got into the land rover and headed back along the way we had come. The troop commander and troop staff sergeant stayed behind with the main bunch of guys and I went off with a Cpl to find what had happened. There it was one truck half on the road, the other half in the ditch with the two guys a little shaken but were ok. But I was still missing one, where the fuck was he; perhaps he had been hurt; all these thoughts were going through my head. Then he appeared walking towards me crouching over as he was walking, I thought he had been hurt so I ran over to him but he was fine. He told me he was walking like that so as not to be seen by the enemy. He was ok but not happy with his co-driver who did not wait for him to get into the vehicle. He said he was half in the cab but lost his footing and fell of the truck, he was covered in mud but was alright.

After living out on the prairie for a week you are starting to stink, you are sweating continuously, and the dust just sticks to you layer on layer. Of course you wash but the water you have is also for cooking as well so you have to be a bit careful with the amount that is used. So you just wash the main areas on your body, which are the armpits, your nuts, of course your arse, and most importantly of all your feet. But always remember to shave first before you do the rest of the body parts.

A day or too later we received an order for us to go and replenish one of the artillery units with water. This detail would need a couple of lads to drive to the artillery's location, and collect their water bowser, which is fitted to the flat bed of a four ton truck. One of the guys would get into their truck and drive it back to base camp and fill it up with fresh water, and then return it to the unit. Before they left I spoke to the lad who would be driving the truck, and told him to drive to our location once he had filled up the bowser.

Later on that day he appeared all nice and clean, he had taken the opportunity of having a shower while he was back in base camp perks of the job I suppose. I climbed onto the top of the water bowser and opened up the hatch and there it was staring at me about 3000 litres of crystal clear water. This was an opportunity I was not going to miss or give up; it was something that had to be done. The lads were standing there bollock naked apart from their combat boots and their towels. The army works on rules, and there was rules for what was about to happen and they were very simple. There was to be no soap or shampoo used when inside the bowser, there is to be a maximum of six at any one time in the bowser, and you have got twenty minutes so get in there.

What a sight for sore eyes it was funny as hell, to see grown men bobbing around inside a water bowser, and then popping up through the hatch and trying to get out, while others were trying to get in. The outside of the bowser was roasting due to it being so bloody hot, so everyone was burning there arses and other parts of their anatomy when trying to climb down and of the vehicle. I had already been in and was getting myself dried when the troop commander arrived back from an orders group and was looking a little puzzled as to why three quarters of his men were in a state of undress, and the water bowser driving forward about four feet then braking hard, and was repeating this over and over again.

What is going on sgt Osborne and why is the water bowser stopping and starting, "it's making waves sir" he never answered because he was too busy watching this naked body climb out of the hatch it was the umpire, I don't want to know sgt Osborne. With the lads a lot cleaner and cooler I took a look at the water and closed the hatch, and told the driver to tell someone at the other end that you think the water back at base camp where you filled up is contaminated and needs to be looked at. The unit never asked for an immediate replenishment so they must have used the water for cooking and to wash in but we never found out and they never complained. But what I do know is that I gained a lot of respect from all the lads in the troop.

With the exercise finished and all the top brass happy and pleased with themselves, we had three days to get these vehicles cleaned, serviced, and ready for the hand over to the next battle group, that were due in over the next couple of days. Everyone worked there balls of to get this completed on time and the reason, R & R (REST AND RECOUPERATION). We all had five days off, to do what we wanted, and to go where we wanted. Some of the lads went to Montana (USA), some went to the Banff and the Lake Louise area, and some went down to the town of Medicine Hat.

The town is about twenty kilometers away so we needed transport to get there and back, so we brought a car. This car is handed down to the next battle group for a price, and when you leave you sell it on. It cost something like 500 dollars which was not bad between six of us, and it was massive inside. It had a big bench seat in the front, column gear change, a powerful engine, and a loud exhaust, and of course six lads that wanted to party. We all took turns in driving this beast, so there was no drinking that night for the driver only soft drinks, but as a bonus the driver's food bill was paid for by the rest of the lads.

There was this particular bar we used to go into, and it had everything, girls dancing on stage scantily dressed, the mechanical bull ride, lots of girls to talk to, and it had a great atmosphere. The bar was huge and the beers just flowed and flowed, then it was the shooting of the shots, and if you were still standing you would take on the bull to the delight of the crowd. We never disappointed the crowd they just loved watching macho men get thrown into a heap on the floor, nobody lasted long on the bull but it was a lot of fun.

I asked the bar staff one day where are all the local men, as there doesn't seem many about. Most of them go away logging for a month at a time, and some are due back soon anyway. That was the reason why there were so many women around the bar, I am not sure how many were single but they all seemed to be available. After a couple of nights of being in this bar you get to know a lot of the faces and you're made to feel welcome. And of course the bar wants your money and the amount we were spending was madness so a big grin and a hi lads from the bar staff is worth every bit of effort. The last night of our five days of freedom and we were in the bar and a few of us were hitting on a couple of the girls. It was my turn to get the drinks in so up to the bar I went and ordered the round.

The barmen put the drinks onto a tray for me and started to talk to someone who was standing behind me. I thought it a bit strange as he was looking over my head while talking to this person. I paid for the drinks and picked up the tray and turned around, and came face to face with a beer belly. As I looked up and up I realised the loggers must have arrived back in town, I am six foot tall and fairly well built but up against this guy I was a midget. These guys are not just big guys they are huge men. I apologised to the man for being in his way and for actually breathing, and made my way away from the bar by ducking under his armpit. I noticed the guys had already moved to another part of the bar well away from the women, what a life saving move.

For the last four days we had been talking to these women and looking after them when it came to the drinks bill and all of a sudden these huge men were sat in our chairs, talking to our women. But who cared we were alive, and we had all our limbs still attached. We finished our beers and said our goodbyes and got our arses back to the safety of the camp. The next morning with everything packed we made our way to the big bird that would take us back to Germany. Thank you Canada I had a great time and will see you again.

CHAPTER TWENTY-NINE

After a week's leave it was back to work, and we were preparing for another exercise which was taking place the following week. This was to last for three weeks and then it was a quick weeks Regimental training, and this would be followed by Northern Ireland training. With the exercise completed and the boring Regimental training out of the way, it was head first into the Ireland training. This was going to be another 4 months tour and would take in the Christmas and new year. Most of the lads took this on the chin, it was not great but that's life and shit happens. It was different for the wives and they were pretty well pissed off with the thought of their old man being away over Christmas.

There were a few wives that did make life a little unpleasant for their husbands. They would say things like (well that's typical fucking army that is) or it would be (I might as well be at my mums, what's the point of being married your always away). This really pissed me off for two reasons. A soldier has to be 100% focused on the job he is carrying out, if he is not and his mind is elsewhere, then mistakes happen, and people will get hurt. The other reason is (that if it was not for the husbands then the wife would not be living the good life in a foreign country).

The divorce rate in the Army was the highest out of the three services, they say that it takes a special kind of women to be married to a soldier and that is very true. You can be away a lot of the time depending what unit you are serving with. The unit that we are in now, you would expect to be away four to five months a year. You could double that if you got a Northern Ireland tour. The guys could handle it a lot better than the wives, and the reason was they had all there mates around them 24/7. It was not in a soldiers make up, or the macho thing to do and that was to show any emotions towards his wife. Turning around and saying something like god I really miss my wife or I would rather be at home with her then be out here with you lot just never happened. It was ok to say that you missed your kids, but to say you're missing the wife no way.

The married guys would do the macho thing like go to the bar and hang out with the lads, and say things like, I cannot wait to get home and shag the mrs, or she will be bowed legged after I finish with her when I get back.

But the wives, what could they do or say, I'm sure they never sat around at coffee mornings saying god I cannot wait for the old man to get back and give me a good seeing too, because I am gagging for it. No they were at home looking after the kids feeding them, keeping them entertained while trying to lead some kind of a normal life, and a lot of the time there was nobody for them to talk to. They also had the constant worry that the old man may come home inside a wooden box. Yes there was the wives club for the wives to go to maybe once or twice a week for a cup of tea and a chat but they were very clicky. It was normally run by the RSMs wife and the COs wife would show a bit of interest now and again. Now the RSMs wife would turn up with all her friends i.e. the other SSMs and SNCO wives. Now these wives would dress for the occasion not over the top but smarter than they would normally dress. So when the young wives came into the coffee morning dressed in there blue Ron Hills and trainers a few comments would get whispered around.

There was more jealousy between the wives over the ranks of their husbands then there was between the guys themselves. We would honestly say well done congratulations to who ever got promoted and it was meant. On the other hand the wives would give it, why are you not promoted, you're better than him it's not fair and all that crap. So a lot of the junior ranks wives would keep away from using the wives club, and try and sort out there problems by themselves or with the help of the wives whose husbands held the same rank as there's.

Training was almost complete and for those that had completed tours of N I before it was like an intense refresher course, but we were taking quite a few red arses with us (first timers) and that was a small concern. You had to drum it into them that this was not a game and it was for real when we got out there. There were people out there who had nothing better to do then blow your head off it was as simple as that, nothing else mattered to these fanatics. The other problem we had was on arrival in Ireland a number of the guys were going out to remote border areas where they would be supporting the infantry detachments. So we had the task of trying to match up those with experience with those with a little experience, and hope that they would learn very quickly.

The day came for the advance party to leave; this would normally include the SSM, along with the SQMS, the pay sgt, and of course the armourer, along with about 10 to 15 other ranks. These would arrive about one week before the main party and their job was to sign and take over everything from the outgoing unit. All the stores had to be accounted for down to the last round, the accommodation had to be checked i.e. sheets, pillars, check the mattresses for piss stains. All the vehicles had to be checked over and signed for, so a Reme representative was on the advance party as well. But it had its perks being on the advance party you could get the best bed spaces for a start and take your time settling in. The best perk of all was that the guys from the outgoing unit would always have things for sale. You would buy anything that would make your stay out there a lot more comfortable; we all need our creature comforts.

CHAPTER THIRTY

The first couple of days are always hectic whenever you arrive somewhere new and Ireland is no different. Getting people to where they needed to be at the right time does not always work out. The transport can break down or it turns up late for some reason. Another problem that happens is the units that you are going to give manpower too have changed their personnel requirement and this is different to the requirement you were told in Germany.

The main reason that this happens is because the unit that you are supporting, may have been given some additional commitments and the long and short of it is they need extra man power and basically we have to supply it simple as that. This happened to us just as we arrived a unit we were supporting down on the border informed us that they needed two extra guys for two months, so it was a case of robbing Peter to pay Paul. Well that's a good start let's hope it gets better as the weeks roll on. These things as we say are sent to try us and try us they do, but it's all part of the job. When that problem gets sorted out there will always be another one waiting in the line to challenge you.

The tour was going well everyone was finally in there right place and we all knew what we were doing to some extent. Those personnel that we had detached to the outside units were very happy and the units were also happy with the man power they had been given. The lads working in Belfast were doing a good job covering all the daily tasks that had to be met. There are a lot of military units dotted around Northern Ireland and they need to get supplies delivered to them daily. They cannot just walk into a shop and do their shopping, so it is up to us to go to the stores depot and collect what they needed and then deliver the goods. This was not an easy job because getting stuck in traffic while sitting inside a large green army vehicle is not the best thing to be doing in Ireland. The obvious problem is you do not blend in with your surroundings and you really do stick out like a sore thumb compared to the rest of the traffic. But that was the only way it could get done back then, and so we crossed our fingers and toes and just got on with it.

The Divis flats was a notorious place for past and present violence and many people had come to grief there, be it civilians or military so it was not a great place to hang out. The military had an operation room on the top floor of one of these blocks which gave them a bird's eye view of certain areas. These people needed to get supplied as well but this could only be done by air. It was way too dangerous and impractable to do this on the ground. The military had occupied the whole top floor of this particular block of flats but all the other floors still had civilians who were living in the flats below them. So walking in the bottom door with Tesco's bags in each hand and catching the lift to the top floor was not an option for us. Things had the habit of falling down from the floors above and causing people a lot of pain in the past, so anything they needed had to be delivered onto the roof.

I was a qualified Helicopter Handler (H H) a course I had done just so I could get another course under my belt never thinking I would ever have to put into practice what I had been taught, but the army is full of surprises. The job of the heli handler is to make sure that the helicopter has a clear and safe approach to where he needs to land, or to drop of his under slung load.

The ground has to be clear of anything that could fly up and damage the aircraft when it is coming into land, taking off or hovering. Power lines and overhead cables have to be noted and given to the operations room as soon as you had completed your recce. The pilot will sometimes take a bit of notice of you but he is more concerned in flying the aircraft.

It's the load master who you work with and he is the guy who hangs out the side door and relays your instructions to the pilot. If I make a signal for them to move to the right then he would tell the pilot to move to the right. They are relying on you to get them into the right place and onto the ground safely do what needs to be done and then get the hell out of there.

The land rover dropped me off outside the block of flats and I quickly ran inside the building with my escort. The lift was on its way down from the top floor they had seen us arrive, these boys could see and hear everything that went on in those flats. The lift door opened and I was staring into the barrel of a 9mm pistol just inches from my head passwords were exchanged and I got into the lift and was on my way to the top floor. My escort had not got into the lift and was safely back in the land rover, which was well on its way back to camp.

The view was amazing you could see for miles and miles all over Belfast but I was not there for the sightseeing tour or the view there was a helicopter due, in about thirty minutes and I had to get my shit together. With my helmet on and with the radio attached I went up onto the roof.

What a strange feeling there I was standing on the roof of one of these blocks that made up the Divis flats, and while I was looking around at the wonderful scenery Twenty floors up I was thinking what am I doing here. There I was looking straight into the windows of the other flats in the other blocks, so if I could see them then they could see me, but I had nowhere to go.

There in the distance was the helicopter and it was on its way the dot got bigger and bigger as it drew nearer. My headset came to life all of a sudden with the voice of the pilot asking for a situation report. (sit rep). Area cleared for receiving I told him and after a small pause I said "and all quite at the moment" an answer came back from who I don t know but they said (that's comforting to hear) I had a little chuckle to myself. I could see the aircraft clearly now but could not work out what the load was in the cargo net, then I realised it was a chest freezer. Before I knew it the helicopter was hovering in front of me and I was giving the load master all the signals that I needed to give for a safe touchdown. There was a lot of downdraft from the helicopter and at one time I had to crouch down to regain my balance. Twenty floors up and not having much room to move around dealing with the downdraft from the helicopter and not being tied on was a perfect recipe for disaster. Having hit the metal hook with my spike stick (discharging the buildup of electricity) I was under the aircraft and had unhooked the cargo net. Moving back I gave the thumbs up to the loadmaster showing that the load was detached. I checked the sky around me and it was clear, I then gave the all clear to the pilot and away he went, job well done. A few of the guys had been in position watching the surrounding area whilst this was all going on and had now gathered the freezer. After getting the cargo net of one of the lads opened the lid only to find it full of frozen food. There was no way we could lift this down two flights of stairs to the ops room. So there we were on top of the notorious Divis Flats in full view of anyone who wanted to take a shot at us whilst we emptied the freezer. There were bags of chips peas, burgers, fish ,you name it, it was in there. With the freezer emptied it was time to get it down below which we managed, then it was up and down the two flights of stairs collecting all the food that was left on the roof. With all the food collected and freezer plugged in and working we sat down and chilled out. An hour later I was back on the roof with the old freezer. And I mean "old "and waiting for chopper to arrive. Here it come one of the lads shouted out, and there it was in the distance and on its way. I took up my position and got the chopper hovering about six feet above the freezer. Then I went under the aircraft, climbed on to the freezer and after spiking the hook I lifted up the metal ring which is attached to the cargo net and tried to attach it to the aircraft but it was to high informed the load master that he had to get lower and then I saw him looking under the belly of the aircraft, where he could see that they needed to get lower. It's some experience crouched under a helicopter which is about two feet above your head and trying to attach a load. Finally I got the hook on, jumped down and stood in front of the aircraft. Giving the all clear signal to the pilot he started to lift the load, after checking the load was hanging correctly, I gave the signal that all was well and within seconds he was flying over Belfast with a knackered fridge freezer under its belly.

CHAPTER THIRTY-ONE

Christmas and New Year came and went and before we all knew it, we were looking at a couple of weeks left of our tour and then we would be handing over to the next advance party. It's a great feeling knowing there's only a few days left but you have to stay 100% switched on. It's at these times when you can become a little too casual and blasé and let your guard down and before you know it bang there's an accident.

I had seven more days to cross of my chuff chart and then it would be complete and I would be going home the following day. I got called into the ops room where I was told there was another job to be done on top of the Divis flats. For fucks sake you're joking aren't you far from it was the reply, and it's for tomorrow morning. To say I was pissed off would have been an understatement but I knew there was no one else to do it. That morning I was up early and on top of the flats for 0800 hrs., as requested and I waited and waited only to be told that the detail was cancelled.

Three days to push and there I was in an unmarked car wearing civilian clothing and driving to a location outside of Belfast.

It was another helicopter job and this time it was extracting military personnel of the ground and taking them straight to the airport. I found the exact location of where the pickup was to be and started to set up the equipment. This was going to be a night time extraction involving about thirty men. An Approach Angle Indicator (AAI) is used for night time work, it works like this. The pilot is flying to your location but there are a lot of trees surrounding you so you help the pilot by setting up the AAI. When he is on the correct angle of approach he will see a green light being omitted from the AAI If he is to low he will see an orange light and if to high he will see a red light and so he can adjust accordingly. Having set this piece of equipment up all I could do now was wait.

Night had fallen over the area and it was a little eerie I must admit especially sat there on my own. There was twenty minutes to go before the chopper was due and I had not seen or heard a soul. My head set was on but everything was quite there was not even any traffic coming over the radio. Sitting in the dark and straining my eyes for even the slightest movement was starting to do my head in. Then there was a tap on the passenger side window I turned to the side so fast my head nearly came off, and my heart had fallen out of my chest and was now banging away somewhere on the floor. There was a soldier looking in at me with a big smile on his face even though I had a pistol pointing straight at him. I went to open the door but it opened so far and stopped and this head covered in camouflage and combat cream came down to my level and asked "if I was expecting a pick up tonight". I let rip into him by saying "where the fuck have you been I have been here fucking hours and the chopper is due soon. I know was his answer we have been laid over there watching you for some time. With the pleasantries out of the way I asked where his guys were and had they formed up in the correct way so they can board the helicopter when it arrives yes they are was the answer. Now it was raining and coming down fairly heavy but there was no sign of this bloody helicopter.

Then we could hear it in the distance and the guys broke cover I was very impressed they were everywhere and I had not even seen a thing. Contact was made on the radio and we were rolling no lights were being used and all you could see was this huge shape getting nearer. Had I set up the AAI correctly a thought that flashed through my brain for a brief second? The noise was deafening as it got closer to the ground plus the shit that the down draught kicked up was blinding. I was talking to the load master letting him know he was evenly sat on the ground and that we were ready to load.

A couple of seconds past and I got the all clear for us to start loading. I signaled to the lads to start loading and they started making their way forward and onto the helicopter. Everyone had to pass by me as they made their way onto the helicopter. There was only a couple left to board when I noticed this little white head popping out of this lad's jacket it was a dog. A small little terrier had become good friends with these lads during their time over here and they obviously wanted to carry on that friendship back to wherever they were going.

The lad tried to push its head down to stop me from seeing it but I already had and the guy new I had seen the dog. As he came by me he slowed down, he was expecting me to say sorry know animals and to take the dog of off him. Instead I let him by and said nothing, as he passed he said "cheers mate" and got onto the chopper. I passed onto the load master via the radio the numbers that had boarded his aircraft and he confirmed those numbers were correct plus one small package, even the load master had noticed the dog and had said nothing.

The helicopter then climbed into the air and was gone and I was left alone again. I packed up my kit and got the hell out of there as quickly as possible, we had made enough noise to wake the dead. There are rules upon rules in the army, but sometimes you have to turn a blind eye to certain things so as to make other people happy, anyway what was I meant to do with a dog.

A couple of days later it was our turn to be at the airport and getting to board the goes hommy bird. We had completed the tour with flying colours; we had excelled in certain areas and got great reports back from those units we were supporting down on the border. But finally and most importantly of all, everyone returned home safe and sound

CHAPTER THIRTY-TWO

When you have been away for four months and had a couple of weeks leave, it's always a culture shock to the brain and body when you get back to regimental life. The RSM is on the Sqns back straight away this is par for the course. The RSM thinks because we have been away we have lost all regimental discipline and he needs to straighten us out again. He got onto our SSMs back straight away, moaning about nothing but moaning never the less.
The SSM has got to be seen to be doing something about it so he walks around shouting and waving his stick at people. When he sees the RSM next he tells him it's all sorted out and when this happens the RSM is a very happy man, and tells the CO that he has got the Sqn back in shape.
In reality this is what happens. The SSM gets you on parade and yes he is waving his arms around and pointing his stick and shouting at us, but to no one in particular. This is done for effect as the RSM would be watching from a distance feeling pretty smug with himself, but he cannot hear what the SSM is saying. What our Sergeant Major was really saying was "look lads you know the score the RSM is watching, and it's part of my job to be an arsehole now and then. We had a great tour all of you have done well, and the CO is very pleased with the Sqn, so don't fuck it up and let yourselves down.
The rest of 1987 came and passed without too much excitement a few exercises here and there, a bit of regimental training, anything to keep the lads occupied.
I went and passed an education course (EPC A) which lasted for four weeks; this was a course you needed to pass if you were going to be considered for the rank of a warrant officer. Personnel change all the time within the Sqn, and we had got a new officer commanding and there was a new RSM in the camp.
I knew the RSM from a few years back when he was a SSgt and we got on very well with each other then, so hopefully nothing would have changed. At the time I never realised just how close we would be working together, but I was soon to find out.
It was now May 88 and I was thinking of all the different units which I could get posted to. My three years where nearly up and I had had a good three years. I had not been in any trouble and I had matured slightly and I knew I had done a good job. The RSM calls for me and there I am in his office talking about a new post that the CO wants to create in the regiment. It was his baby, his idea, his train set, and the fact that it would be the first time that anything like this would have been done in the Corps. Good for

him Sir, so why are you telling me, because he wants you to drive the train, was his answer. We sat and talked for a bit it was certainly going to be the biggest challenge of my life, and I also knew that if I did not screw up trying to achieve the old man's ideas then it should stand me in good stead for the future.

I had an interview with the CO and he laid out his plans for what he wanted and expected me to achieve. After the interview I said to the RSM is he really on this planet, or is he smoking drugs. I also got my posting that day, I was posted internally within the regt and it was for a further three more years.

CHAPTER THIRTY-THREE

.The commanding officer had left me with no illusions at all of what he wanted me to achieve. I was to answer to two men and two men only the RSM and the CO. Whatever I needed I would be able to get within reason. I had no barriers in front of me and I was given that much rope, I could have hung myself ten times over. But I was also well aware that everyone of any importance was watching me 24/7.
Induction Troop was the name of the COs train set, and basically I got every new solider straight out of training who was posted to the regt and they would spend at least one week with me. It was a time when training regiments were just churning out soldier's everyday even if they had completed their training or not. It was a numbers game that the army was playing with the MOD. We were receiving lads straight out of training who had failed the basic fitness test, and even some of the lads had missed all there range days because they were sick. More concerning was these young lads were getting posted to an operational unit like this one, and really they had not even completed their basic training.
So when they arrived they were mine, and there were 76 objectives that each individual had to pass before they would be sent to one of the Sqns. They slept in separate accommodation away from the rest of the regt; they did not mix with any of the regt personnel even their lunch meal was collected and brought down to where we were teaching. I had one Corporal and two Lance Corporals and that was the team. Between us we had to turn these lads we were receiving from the training units into half decent soldiers that were then capable of joining an operational Sqn.
The lads would arrive in there ones and twos or sometimes in a group of ten, so it was hard and confusing sometimes to keep on top of who had done what. I had a large board made that showed every objective that had to be completed, and spaces for at least fifty names down the one side. Each time a soldier completed an objective a disc would then be placed alongside his name and under that objective. Sometimes you could be teaching to ten soldiers, and then the next time you may only have three to teach. But they would be all together during the exercise period which lasted two days and a night.
When we started this Induction Troop the commanding officer had said, you would have a maximum of twenty at a time. We had forty eight guys in the troop when he paid us a visit one of his many I might add, and he seemed impressed at what he saw but you can never tell with these fuckers.
We were getting great feedback from the Sqn Commanders as well, they were very happy with what they were getting from us and this obviously

filtered down to the RSM and the CO. I had become detached from the regt by now and from its day to day running and this was something I was missing. But I knew this particular job was not forever and I knew it would not be long before I would be back there.

We had about 2 hours before we were due to leave the barracks for the exercise area when the RSM told me, that I had to go to the airport and pick a new lad up. So my Cpl took charge and deployed for the training area while I drove to the airport. I put his name on a piece of paper and waited for his flight to arrive. He came over a bit sheepish and told me he was the person on the paper. I said to him "I hope you have all your military kit with you because we are going straight on exercise". He did not know if I was joking or what but when I told him to get changed in the toilet he knew I was being serious.

The exercise was very intense and a lot of objectives had to be covered in a short space of time. The lack of sleep affected both us and the soldiers and this had to be managed in the right way. If you make learning fun you will get the full attention from whoever you are teaching so that was what we done.

During the end of the night phase they were told that the staff were going to attempt to enter their location and take one of their men. If we succeeded in doing this then all of you guys are going to do the river crossing. On the other hand if you catch us attempting to get one of your guys then all the staff will do the river crossing. The river crossing was not one of the objectives that had to be completed it was just a bit of fun and nobody wanted to do a river crossing.

Doing something like this you could see the potential leaders amongst them. A couple of them would be saying to the rest of the guys, come on we can stay awake, we will sleep in shifts, and the waters fucking freezing, lets catch one of them come on lads. Out of all the exercises we done while in Induction Troop we got caught twice and true to my word all the staff done the river crossing much to the delight of the lads.

We would get back into barracks on Saturday lunch time where the vehicles had to get washed down and the weapons had to be immaculate and inspected before going back into the armoury. Once everything was done it was free time for the lads. They had to get there washing done, and ironed for Monday mornings inspection, so that did not leave them that much free time but you grab it while you can.

My Cpl had a little scam going on and I turned a blind eye to it. There were no washing machines for the guys to use, so he would charge them a small fee to take their washing home with him. He would say "there's a washing machine and dryer sat in the house doing nothing and I need to get my kit washed, and the wife's not busy this weekend".

So he would load his car up with the guys washing and take it home with him. On Sunday morning he would be back in camp dropping of the lads washing and collecting his fee.

Nearly a year after getting told I was going to run the COs train set I pulled it into the station for the last time. The last of the guys had moved into their Sqns, and Induction Troop was shut down for good. The actual reason for it closing was that the training units had caught up with the numbers game and recruiting figures had shot through the roof (well there's a big surprise). I was sat in the COs office with the RSM and we were talking about what we had achieved in the last year, which was an incredible amount, and of course the ups and the not so many downs. Each soldier that had come through Induction Troop had completed an intense training period, which incorporated 76 objectives which he had to pass and complete within a week.

After the training he was by far a better soldier then what he was when he had first arrived in our opinion. I was very pleased that Induction Troop had worked so well. From the very beginning it was a big challenge, the setting up of the troop, the day to day running of the troop, and finally the closing down part.

I was getting lots of pats on the back and well dones but I always told those who were patting my back, it was a team effort and without those three other guys and their commitment Induction Troop would never have worked.

It may have been the COs idea and his baby, but it was defiantly my train set. I was the driver, the signal man, the guard, and of course the Fat Controller.

CHAPTER THIRTY-FOUR

I was promoted to SSgt (Staff Sergeant) in early April 89, and once again I was posted internally within the regt. I was to take charge of about 40 personnel that specialised in carrying fuel in tankers or in special pods. I was over the moon with getting promoted and I knew my one year in Induction Troop had proved to all those around me, that I had the ability to carry out the majority of tasks that were thrown my way. I have always had a lot of self-confidence, and that is a key factor if you are to progress within the military.
When I was not sure how to do something I always asked and got the advice I needed. Every task that I was given I would think it through a hundred times in my mind before doing it. And finally you need lady luck to be on your side sometimes.
I already knew the OC and the SSM of my new Sqn from my time in Induction Troop, and many of the guys in the Sqn had spent their first week in the regt with me. The problem I had in taking over the fuel troop was I had never worked with fuel before let alone the vehicles that carried the fuel.
I was not Hazmat trained which is a must for anyone who is involved with the handling of fuel. The safety factors that have to be adhered to when pumping or receiving fuel is endless, and when you take these vehicles on exercise it is a completely different ball game.
On the first day in my new job as the troop SSgt I got the troop on parade and after the obligatory inspection I got them formed up in a semi-circle in front of me, and introduced myself. I have always had a friendly and good working relationship with my soldiers. I am a firm believer that if you treat a person with respect you will get the best out of that person, and they will want to work for you plus they will enjoy doing what they do. I have found by taking this approach my job is made so much easier.

I told them that when I am in uniform you will address me as Staff, and when you see me out of uniform i.e. down town, you can call me Steve or Ossie I don't care. This was frowned upon by other SNCOs and SSMs their thinking is, I have earned this rank and so those of lesser rank will always use it regardless if I am in uniform or civvies how sad.
Anyway that was not the way I worked, and up until now it had not done me any harm so why should I change. I told them that I do not hold a grudge and if you get a bollocking from me it's for a reason and after the bollocking, we all go back to the way we were. I have an open door policy

so if you have any problems come and speak to the troop Sgt or me, and do not bottle things up because they will only get worse. And finally I told them all "I have not a clue about how a fuel troop runs, so I will be relying on you all to guide and teach me over the next few weeks.

With the parade over and the men briefed on how I worked and what was expected from them, I went into my new office and started the overhaul. First I made up new vehicle boards which showed the availability, and the history of every vehicle I had in the fleet.

Certain ways of doing things were implemented and some old ones were thrown out. They say a new brush sweeps clean well I had certainly done that. After work I would go home and read about Hazmat, and the different types of fuels, and how these Tankers worked. I was on a TTF (Truck Tanker Fuel) course within the first month, which taught me loads, but more importantly I could now speak with my lads and know exactly what they were talking about it was great.

After two months I was Hazmat as well as TTF trained and I had read every manual that we had, with reference to carrying fuel in tankers or ubres, (Unit Bulk Refueling Equipment) or Pods (Petrol or Diesel) as they were known.

My first exercise had arrived and our role was to have fuel supply sections set up over a very large area, so all the vehicles taking part in the exercise could fill up when they needed to. With all my tankers and pods full it was time move out and learn how different exercising with fuel vehicles actually was. I myself had a land rover and a driver to get around the exercise area and I needed it.

Exercising with fuel vehicles is completely different for example, You are not allowed to put up camouflage netting over the vehicles, as the nets are highly flammable, this was one of the perks of being in a fuel troop. You must always be parked on a hard standing surface and there must be plenty of room for all types of vehicles, from motor bikes to tanks they must be able to fill up safely, it's just like a petrol station.

You must never set up the vehicles next to any water features like a river, a stream or a lake. How cushtie is this for the lads no wonder there was always people trying to get into fuel troop and I thought it was because of me.

This was a totally new way of exercising for me it was so much different from what I knew. My orders would read something like we need fuel vehicles set up here here and also here. But here could mean an area covering five to ten square kilometres. My job was to find a suitable area where a couple of vehicles could set up and be able to discharge there fuel safely to whoever needed it, while complying strictly to all the safety issues i.e. Hazmat and the health and safety regulations.

It was always a race against the clock and there was always something that would stop me from thinking that I had found the perfect area. It could have been there was over head cables directly above us, this is a conservation area, or there is a stream 100 meters away and could get polluted if there was a fuel spillage. It was a constant challenge and to make matters worse, you were being watched continuously by the civil authorities. Once I had found a suitable area for the vehicles I would go back to the exercise area and collect the vehicles that I needed and take them to their new location.

The lads would start setting up straight away, all the hoses that would be used would be laid out and the warning and safety signs were put out at the appropriate distances from the vehicles. While I was watching the guys setting up I could not help but notice how professional they were. They all new there was some great perks in this job but they also knew that one slip up could mean a catastrophic explosion or a major contamination incident. I had to have 100% confidence in all the guys and that was not hard to get after watching them a few times setting up the equipment, they all new the score so I let them get on with it. On a number of times there could be up to five separate locations each one of them pumping fuel so I had to trust them all, as I could not be everywhere at once.

During the exercise my job was very challenging and stressful but it was also very rewarding. To be in a refueling area watching your lads filling up convoys of trucks or tracked vehicles in a professional manner, and sometimes in the eyes of the media is extremely satisfying indeed.

The media would be there because I may have set up the fuel supply route in a small village, so the arrival of military fuel tankers and pods, in the early hours of the morning was big news. Once they got over the shock of seeing and hearing us lot rocking up in their village the locals were always friendly. It was not unusual for the vehicle operators to get showers in these people's homes.

They would get meals cooked for them and of course men in uniform always attracted women. When the convoys were due to come through the town the locals would always know about it. The police would turn up just to show a presence and quite often the photographer from the local paper would be clicking away along with the many onlookers.

A lot of the onlookers asked if they could have their pictures taken with the fuel operators especially the kids, and of course the girls. So me being me allowed this to happen, but it had to be carefully managed. I would take one of the on lookers at a time over to the fuel operator while he was not pumping fuel, and would let them get their photograph taken.

It was against all the rules and regs of the army but what harm was it causing, none at all. It was carefully managed, and the civilians from the village or the town where able to interact with the military. In fact what I was doing was getting better working relationships between the military and the civilian population. Well that's the excuse I would have given if I had got caught.

All the exercises we done basically followed the same routine finding a suitable area, setting up the equipment, and refueling all the exercise vehicles. We would then move onto another area and do it all over again.

Accounting for the fuel was a bit of a headache and it was down to the operators to keep an up to date account of what had been issued. The large tankers would go into the fuel depots and take on 10,000 or 22,000 litres of fuel at a time. Once he had signed for the fuel he would leave the depot and make his way back to the exercise area, or go straight to the re supply area. Once there he would sometimes transfer his fuel into the pod vehicles.

The Pods as they were known as were basically a 4 ton vehicle that had been stripped down and 2 large fuel containers had been placed on the back of the truck. Basically hoses were attached to tanks a few levers were put here and there and a donkey engine fitted to the bed of the truck as well. You would start the donkey engine up and start pumping fuel it was as simple as that.

These Pod vehicles could go deep into the exercise areas and fill up the vehicles while they were still in their locations. They had 4 wheel drive and high and low ratios for the gears, so they could basically go anywhere within reason. There was one drawback with these vehicles you got filthy when operating them, they were always springing leaks and there was always a constant seepage coming from some connection. And finally the donkey engine had a mind of its own, some days it would start and other days it would just turn over and over without firing.

With the exercise finished it was not a case of getting back to camp as quickly as you can and getting the vehicles cleaned, and go home ,oh we wished. We always came back of the exercise with fuel in the pods or in the tankers. This had to be accounted for and taken onto the regiments books. As the regt had its own ground fuel tanks it was then pumped into those as soon as possible.

Once this was completed then we could start the cleaning process and this was a pain in the arse. Different solvents were used to try and clean the spilt fuel off of these vehicles but it was a long process and took ages to complete. Once the vehicles were all cleaned they would have to go to the fuel depot were they would get de- gassed. All the hazardous fumes would be extracted from the tanks and when this was completed you got the de- gassed certificate and that meant it was safe to go ahead and work on the vehicles without breathing in all the fumes.

Supporting other units on exercise with their fuel requirements was the main role of the fuel troop that is not to say that we never played soldiers because we did. If we were not supporting other units in the field then we were on exercise doing our own training with the rest of the squadron or regt.

The squadron had been asked to supply a troops worth of men to go to Canada with an Infantry Regt. With three troops in the squadron for the OC to choose from everyone was hoping he would pick their troop. It was up to the OC to choose who would go and I could not do anything about it or could I.

I had some paper work for the old man to sign fuel receipts, and some other crap, but I had got into the old man's office and I was alone with him. I had got the signatures that I needed and now it was time to work my magic. As I was leaving his office I said to the boss "do they require fuel operators for the exercise in Canada and if so how many would I have to supply".

Amazing he did not know the answer which surprised me somewhat as the boss was always on the ball. I then hit him with "when I was there a couple of years ago they were short on fuel operators, the battle group were told to bring so many but during the exercise they were short. The boss said he would let me know as soon as he found out.

It was not long before I got the call to pop in and see him. I knew I had to keep the pressure on the boss and I was ready for him. According to the exercise instructions staff we need to supply eight fuel operators and a full Cpl who is to be in charge of them. That is not enough sir, take my word for it the lads will be burnt out within a week. Driving, pumping, refueling, 24 hours a day it's asking for an accident to happen sir. Without taking a breath I said send sixteen sir if they are not required to pump fuel then they can do normal soldiering.

At least whoever takes the troop over there will know they have the fat in the system to change operators when they see fit. Remember sir it's a specialist job operating these vehicles so I would suggest sending extra operators. Ok Staff I will run it by the SSM when he gets in.

I had planted the seed of doubt in the old man's mind and with the up most respect for him and the SSM they knew nothing about fuel vehicles. But what they did know was that my troop had never let the Sqn down while supporting other units it was only a matter of time. Then the SSM called me in closed the door and started sniggering to himself. What's wrong I said he started to laugh and then replied, "I've got to give it to you Steve, you're a clever bastard and the OC is concerned about how many fuel ops he needs to send to Canada? So he has decided that it would be wise to send your troop to Canada. I never said a word to the lads and at the end of the day I held a parade (which was very unusual for me) and informed the troop that they were on the way to Canada. This news was greeted with a lot of cheering and hugging a few of the lads said "we knew you would get us this tour, cheers staff."

Again Canada was brilliant from the minute we landed the lads were on the case and they kept it up continuously throughout the entire exercise. One small incident happened but we managed to keep it in house. One of the lads was driving a large fork lift truck at night and we were moving to our new location. All of a sudden I saw these head lights facing towards the night sky and I knew straight away that a vehicle had turned over.

When I got there the fork lift was on its side and the driver was stood there swearing at it. Funny as hell he was actually blaming the vehicle for the accident and not himself. A couple of our vehicles were fitted with a crane which was seated behind the cab, so within minutes we had some lifting strops around the fork lift and lifted it back onto its wheels. A quick inspection of the vehicle and we were on our away again. There was no damage done to the vehicle nothing that a bit of paint wouldn't hide and most importantly of all nobody got hurt. Even the umpire was impressed with how we dealt with that incident and never reported it.

A great R + R was had by everyone and there was some interesting stories being passed around. We climbed onto the plane and settled down for the long journey back to Germany.

The OC received glowing reports from the battle group commander which filtered down to the CO and RSM. He congratulated the troop for a job well done and we were sent on a week's leave. I had a few things to catch up with before I went on leave and I was in the office when the OC came in and we started chatting about this and that. He then asked me "in your opinion staff could you have coped with just eight fuel operators out there" No Sir not a chance.

September 1990 and out of the blue I was told to report to the RSM I was not told why, it's just that he wants to see you like yesterday. So down I went and waited outside his door still trying to work out why he wanted to see me. Out he came and said come on follow me and we made our way to the COs office. He tapped the door and in we went I saluted and was told to relax. Congratulations staff I have a posting order here for you it has just arrived by fax. Also I have the privilege of being the first person to congratulate you on your Promotion to Warrant Officer Class 2.

Well my heart fell out my arse I remember saluting and saying ok sir will do, and the RSM saying will do what. It took my brain a second or two to quickly sort everything out and get back to the real world. Talk about being over the moon I thanked the CO and the RSM and asked when do I take up my new appointment. You are to report to your new squadron and take over the duties of the SSM as soon as possible. The CO told me that I was relieved of all duties with the Sqn as of now, and I recommend you get on your way in a couple of days and be their first thing on Monday morning. That gave me five days to get my kit sorted out drive to the UK and report to my new unit.

One small problem I had was that I had a wife and two children to think about and a married quarter to hand back. Just get your arse there for Monday morning the RSM will sort out the rest. I went back to the Sqn and said my goodbyes to the lads and thanked them all for their support and told them to behave themselves. A quick hand shake with the OC was followed by a couple of words of advice from the SSM and I was on my way.

I had spent five years in a Regiment which was known as a penal regiment amongst the RCT lads and had enjoyed every minute of it. Yes it was hard work a lot of the time and you spent a lot of time away from the family. I remembered my conversation with that officer from manning and records back in Berlin, and him saying to me Cpl Osborne you have a good career in front of you, do not waste it. I had arrived at the regt as a Cpl and five years later I was taking up the top posting for a SSM to hold within the RCT. I had proved to everyone in the regt and in the Ivory Towers that I was an outstanding soldier but most of all I had proved it to myself, and that was very important to me.

CHAPTER THIRTY-FIVE

My office was the first office as you entered the Sqn headquarters, and that meant I saw everyone coming and going. The office was a fair size, a large desk for me, a table in the middle of the room with two arm chairs either side, a couple of book cabinets and the obligatory filling cabinet. I sat at my desk surrounded by paper work there were memos to write and files on top of files waiting to get signed off. And on top of this I had to learn what the role of the squadron was and pretty fast too. So during the day I was at work getting to know people and stamping my authority on the squadron in how I wanted things to be done. In the evening I would be sat at home pouring over manuals and trying to understand who we supported and what roll we played in the big picture.
I thought I was fit until I came here these guys were like racing snakes, be it on the flat ground or up hills so that was something else I had to address. After about a month I was up to speed with most of the men and I knew the role of the squadron but most importantly I had the respect of the lads and the SNCOs.
The first Gulf war was raising its ugly head and there were a lot of rumours going around about what units would be going out there. We were away in Plymouth on a squadron training exercise for a week when the OC called me into his room. Sergeant Major the squadron has been ear marked to go to the gulf can you get the men on parade, that was all he said but he was grinning from ear to ear. Well beat me with a fucking great stick until I say stop this was great news for the squadron. With the men told it was a case of an early return to barracks and start planning for the deployment.
It was now the beginning of November and the boss had just returned from his latest briefing as he walked by my office he looked in and smiled, and said "Sergeant Major my office please". I just knew he had our deployment date and all the pieces of the jigsaw that had been missing all the guessing would soon be over who, what, when, how now it was time for the facts.
We are to deploy to the Gulf with a Sqn strength of 167 Personnel. The Advance party will leave on the 27 December followed by the main party which will leave on the 3rd of January 1991. After he finished he just looked at me and said "I know what you're going to say" I knew he was holding something back I knew the boss to well and he was crap at trying to hide things. Sir we only have about 120 personnel within the Sqn, and that's including our chefs and Reme personnel.
So what unit is going too top us up so we can get our full quota of

personnel? He was still staring at me with his pale blue eyes when he said "THE BAND".

The fucking band your joking Sir what band what do you mean the band, it's the RCT band Sergeant Major. No way Sir we can't go to war with a load of trumpeters and fucking bugle players, playing fucking tunes in the desert. They arrive on Monday morning and you have about six weeks to get them ready, oh fucking brilliant Sir.

Sir these guys are not soldiers in the sense that they run around on exercises and do active service. During a war their role would be carrying out the duties of a stretcher bearer, you know picking up the dead and wounded and not fighting the enemy. And they sit in clubs and halls at night playing tunes to old people. Very true Sergeant Major but from next Monday they are all yours

CHAPTER THIRTY-SIX

. After working through the weekend with my SNCOs setting up training programs and getting accommodation ready for another forty or fifty man, and also letting the master chef know that from Monday there will be another fifty mouths to feed. We had also made a list for things to do on Monday morning like the booking of ranges, and also the booking of the training wings facilities and much much more.
There it was the coach had just arrived outside the Sqn HQ and I said to the OC well here we go let's see what they are like. Standing there with the boss watching them getting off the bus was like watching a bus load of tourists who had just arrived at their hotel. Some had problems getting of the bus with their bags, their bag straps were getting caught on the doors. There holdalls were not military holdalls because they had not been issued any so what am I looking at, bags of every different colour known to man were being unloaded from the coach. What a fucking shambles there was no one taking charge or organising anything, they were just milling around looking for a tour rep.
Well it was not long before they met the tour rep and I was not wearing a Thompsons badge, I let rip it was like a nuclear bomb had gone off they did not know whether to stand still or get into three ranks one guy even got back on the coach. I was prowling around like a bear with a sore head shouting and swearing, and every time I looked at anyone of them there was something else for me to rant about. They were a shower of shit and I told them that in no uncertain terms, I held nothing back.
Then one of my staff sergeants informed me that the weapons that they had brought down with them were the old SLR. The SLR (self-loading rifle) was the standard issued weapon throughout the Army for many years but had been super seeded by the SA 80 about three years earlier. So that was another fit I had even your weapons are out of fucking date, you can keep them and take them with you but the rounds we get issued with now won't fit the fucking things.
The OC had managed to take the officer of the band well away from the chaos that was happening around him, most likely to give him a coffee or a cup of tea. Then this rather tall thin man made his way over to me and introduced himself. Hello I am the sergeant major of the band and these are my men. I did not even look at him all I said was, "you was and they are mine now", and walked away.
It was very rude of me to behave like that and not the way to do things but he had been standing around and had done nothing and it had taken him ten minutes to come over and introduce himself I did not even know they

had a SSM. Then one of the bandsmen called the SSM by his first name, who in turn answered him using his first name. That was the straw that broke the camel's back. I left the SQMS to take them to their accommodation and I made my way up to the OCs office with their SSM behind me.

The officer of the band was still in the OCs office so I went to my office and phoned him, and told him we need to speak and it needs to be now. I told him what had happened down stairs and that the officer and the SSM of the band need to know that we are running this show and not them. The OC agreed with me and left my office and took them both into his office and explained to them the facts of life.

The two of them even had the balls to go over to the commanding officer and moaned to him about what they had been told. Myself and the OC were both summoned over to the COs office and the two of them were still in there. The RSM was in there as well, oh what a lovely little gathering I said. The CO just threw me a look he was a man that did not mince his words he said it as he saw it, and always spoke with calmness in his voice. Gentleman there is to be only one officer commanding and only one Sergeant Major in the Sqn that is deploying to the Gulf, and Major ---- and SSM Osborne already hold those positions is that understood. I expect both of you to give them as much support as you can that is all gentleman Thank You.

CHAPTER THIRTY-SEVEN

The training was extremely hard for all the members of the band but give credit where credit is due they put everything they could muster into it. They were constantly getting bollocked by me and I never let up, I would hound them both day and night. There was that much training to cover we even had to work in the evenings which pissed my lads of a tadge. But as each day passed they got better and better and the bollocking's got less and less.

It was early December and a lot of the training had been completed and I was sat having a chat with the OC and all the SNCOs. There was nobody in that office who could fault their commitment and enthusiasm we had thrown everything at them and so far they were all still standing. Ok they were not perfect there fitness still had to be worked on, and to get them to think like soldiers and not like bandsman was proving a little difficult.

These guys have been behaving like civilians for years, the only difference was that they wore a uniform and that was all. They played in civilian clubs; they had a booking sheet as long as your arm dates for this venue appearances at the town hall and so on. It was not their fault at all it was the MODs fault for allowing this to happen, and then the powers to be send them to a top operational unit like ours and expect us to bring them up to scratch.

The band also had a few oldies with them, these were Cpls who were in their late thirties to early forties so these had to be treated a little bit different. As a Cpl you will be a section commander and have about twelve men in your charge, which will be looking at you for leadership and guidance. There was not to be any segregation between the soldiers of the band and the soldiers of the sqn. All the guys had integrated well with each other which was great and that was what we wanted, but I knew that some of my original lads will be under the command of some of these old Cpls from the band.

They trained the same as everyone else but they did struggle with their fitness. I explained to them that that is not a major problem at the minute it will get better, but it's your leader qualities that I want to see and how you react when under pressure that's was my main concern. All of them were in agreement and understood that it was very important for them to win over the lads that they were going to command.

We had a forty eight hour exercise that had been put into the training programme, not really ideal but it was a must for the entire bandsman whose last exercise would have been during their basic training. But the main reason was to put the Cpls from the band under a lot of pressure and to see how they perform. Overall they done very good of course there was cock ups and mistakes made, but that is why we have exercises so we can correct and learn from the mistakes that are made, in a peace time environment. The feedback I got from the lads was encouraging with regards to the senior Cpls and from what I had seen I was more at ease now.

Christmas was approaching fast and with the last of the training completed all that was left to do was get the lads away for their Christmas break. The OC had a chat with them on parade and thanked them for their commitment and the dedication they had all given towards there training. They had been taken out of there comfort zone blowing trumpets, and banging drums, and thrown into a situation which was alien to all of them plus they had to come to terms with a lunatic of a Sergeant Major.

I wished them all a merry Christmas and echoed the boss's remarks and told them that there was a you and us at the start of the training, but now I am proud to say with all honesty that we are a sqn of 167 men. Make sure you get your arses back here after your leave. I will not be here because I am on the advance party but I have got big ears and I will find out if any off you are late reporting back, now fuck of and I will see you all out there

CHAPTER THIRTY-EIGHT

We took 167 military personnel out to the Gulf and we returned with every one of them. It was a very satisfying for me as a Sergeant Major being able to take all those lads out to a hostile area and return with all of them. There are not that many SSMs who get this chance so I knew I was very fortunate. There have been many books wrote about the Gulf War and their stories so I won't bore you but I would like to share two incidents with you all.

It was the early hours of the morning and apart from the guards who were hopefully awake the rest of us were asleep, when all of a sudden the alarms started going off. When I say alarms I am referring to the ones that tell you if there is a nerve gas or something similar in your area. I fell into my NBC suit and gas mask and got my arse out of the tent. While I was trying to get to grips and find out what was happening I noticed this figure staggering around with his arms straight out in front him. It was like watching Frankenstein walking about. I got over to him and turned him around so he was facing me his respirator was fitted correctly which was a good thing, but he was putting his hands all over my head and face, as if he was trying to feel who I was.

"Sergeant major," "Sergeant Major is that you?", "yes it is" I answered, "thank fuck !I cannot see a thing, help me please." He was not showing any signs of nerve agent poisoning, so I dragged him into the Ops Wagon and told them to look after him while I went back outside to see what was happening. We eventually found out that one of our aircraft while returning to base had dumped some fuel and that's what set of the alarms. With everything back to some sort of normality I went back to the Ops wagon to see how Frankenstein was doing.

There he was sat in the corner on a chair and drinking a cup of tea. Taken back a bit I asked what had happened and why was you impersonating a fucking mummy. He said "Sir I cannot see without my glasses" but you can see me now with your glasses on so wear them all the time you tit". You don't understand Sir, fucking right I don't understand. I don't understand why you are sat down drinking tea, and I'm stood here soaking with sweat after running around the location for an hour, so explain to me.

He explained he needs normal glasses to see with but he cannot wear his normal glasses when he has his respirator on. He needs a different set of glasses that can fit into his respirator and these never turned up while he was back in the UK so you see Sir I am blind when I put my gas mask on.

For fuck sake I said to the OC we now have a mole on the books what's next. All credit to this lad he had come out on an operational tour knowing the chances of getting a gas attack were good. He had not received his glasses which he needed for his respirator so he could see. Imagine going to war and having that constant worry in the back of your mind, but he did and he was out here with us. He also knew if he had told anyone about this problem while we were in the UK he would not have travelled to the Gulf with the sqn.

The perfect remedy to solve this problem was a simple one really; he was to become the driver of the Recon vehicle. The thinking behind this was easy if we were out recceing and was subject to a gas attack, then at least I or the second in command could drive the vehicle and mole could sit in the back. If we are back in the location and we get a gas attack then the mole goes straight to the Ops wagon if he can find it.

One particular day we had been out on a recce and were making our way back to base camp. Myself and the 2nd in command had momentarily dozed off in the vehicle, thus leaving mole our trusty driver all alone at the wheel. I was awoken by the voice of the 2 i/c asking where we were, only to hear our driver say I'm not sure Sir. Not fucking sure what do you mean I'm not sure was my reaction. Well it all seems the same sir the roads and the dessert, I think we are lost.

The Sat Nav was not working that well either, it was only picking up two satellites and it needed three, so it was having problems trying to locate where we were. We drove around for a couple of minutes looking out for anything that would give us a clue to where we were. We finally worked out where we were and so we started to make our way back to camp. The 2 i/c asked mole to turn right but mole being mole turned left instead and carried on driving as if nothing was wrong.

That was it I had had enough I told mole to stop the vehicle and I made my way around to the driver's side. Mole was sat in the driver's seat with a blank expression on his face and said yes Sir. Get out of the vehicle mole and take all your kit out, he did as he was told, and once he had all his kit with him he started to make his way to the back of the vehicle. Where are you going mole I asked, I am getting into the back of the jeep Sir, your bloody going nowhere mole get over here.

Then I gave him the directions he needed to follow if he wanted to get back to camp. I told him you don t listen to the directions given to you when you are driving, so let's see if you listen to the directions given to you now that you are walking. I then climbed into the driver's seat and slowly drove away leaving mole standing there all alone with his kit at his feet and obviously in some kind of shock. The 2 i/c was also in shock as well as to what he had just witnessed, but I explained to him that we were in a safe area and everything would be ok, and hopefully mole will have learnt from this little exercise.

Mole did indeed make it back to camp unharmed he was very hot and tired, but had proved to us and himself that he can listen to directions that are given to him. Our mole became an excellent driver after that little exercise he remembered where we were going and where we had been and the most important thing of all he got his left and right sorted out.

If Mole had never made it back to camp that day I think I would have had a major problem in explaining that one away to the higher authorities. I am still in contact with mole via a social network and we still laugh about these two incidents twenty two years on.

CHAPTER THIRTY-NINE

Everything was getting back to normal now in the camp our stint in the Gulf War was now a distant memory and the lads from the band had gone back to playing their music at different venues across the country. I often wondered if the guys from the band actually missed being in a working unit and playing soldiers.

One of the main roles of the Sqn was that each person had to be trained in the art of Artic Warfare. This would mean going to Norway for a couple of months (January - March) and carry out Winter Warfare Training in sub-zero conditions. As I had never done anything like that before it was something that I was looking forward to doing. But we were only in May and there were a couple of overseas exercises taking place in which we were to be involved in, so the thought of going to Norway was put firmly and squarely to the back of my mind.

Italy was our next point of call and it was to be an infantry type of exercise with a few other countries taking part and of course the host country Italy was involved. We were still all full of ourselves after the Gulf war and the professionalism was being shown constantly amongst the men. This made mine and the other SNCOs jobs a lot easier and we could concentrate on the planning and the admin side of the exercise.

Myself and the SQMS along with a couple of lads were on our way to Italy we were the advance party. The main party would follow us in a few days' time. The exercise was taking place right down in the south of Italy where there seemed little human life in fact I think I saw more wild dogs then humans on my down to the exercise area.

The base camp was a tented camp and there must have been at least sixty tents each of which could accommodate eight men and their equipment set up all over this huge area. After being allocated our tents we then had a walk around to familiarise ourselves with the location. The cookhouse was not hard to find it was the only marque in the area and could hold a couple of hundred men at a time. The toilets were the plastic porter loo type and there was loads of them scattered around the area and at the moment they were still pretty clean, but let's see after a week or so. And of course the bar, well in fact a few bars were starting to spring up. Each country had been designated their own areas and within that area they had there sleeping and living accommodation, toilets, washrooms etc., and of course they put up their own bars.

The camp was buzzing now with hundreds of soldiers and the exercise was due to start in a couple of days' time. But there was a small problem that was going around the camp and it was not taking any prisoners. People were shitting themselves all over the camp, you could be talking to someone and then in a second or two he would be off running to the toilets and would fail to make it. I was in the Ops room when I felt a little rumble in my stomach, ok I thought, don't panic just leave and go to the toilet. It was then that I felt the back of my legs were all of a sudden wet. Yes, I had shit myself and I had not even tried, what a state to get into. So the whole camp had gone down with the shits and it was impossible to get your clothing clean.

Military and civilian medics worked together to sort this out and sort it out they did. After a couple of days we were all a lot better whatever it was it had gone thankfully. Two days of eating boiled rice three times a day, along with loads of water this was the only fluid we were allowed to have.

The exercise was put back by a couple of days but it soon got underway and to be honest it was great to get out of that admin area. Working with different nationalities had its problems during the exercise, they all do things differently, and some are conscripts like the Italians. So trying to get them to dig trenches and stand in them all night is near enough impossible. These lads are not professional soldiers and they get paid a very small amount each day, so it was a challenge to get them to do any soldiering. They also get Grappa (type of snaps) in there ration packs, and as they are always eating, so they are always drinking, say no more.

The exercise went well and we were all back in camp and getting the clean-up phase done. As soon as this was completed and everybody was happy then we had a bit of down time three days off. It was on one of these days that myself and about ten guys went down town well it was more like a village but very nice and peaceful. The lads were well aware on how they should behave while out drinking, so I never really worried about it.

I was standing at the bar getting a round in when this very attractive female came up and started talking to me. Well I was straight in there cock on head, and started a conversation straight away. I took the beers back to the table and got a few comments from the lads with reference to the lady I was chatting to. After a while the women wanted us to leave the bar and go for a wander. I told the lads I was leaving and that they were to behave themselves, and to make sure they get back to camp.

Hundred metres away from the pub and there we were getting down to it and things were going great, until I slipped my hand up her skirt and got a handful of Balls. I froze and just starred at her, or him, or it, and time just stood still. I instinctively took a step back, and he or her said don t hit me. I just walked away and went back to the bar and the looks of disbelief on the faces of the guys were a picture when I walked back in. After telling them what had happened they were ready to rip the place apart, but there was no need for that, it was my entire fault, so don't worry forget it.

The door opened and he/she walked back into the bar and just carried on as if nothing had happened. After I had sunk a few more beers I started to get really worried about myself. I caught myself a few times looking over at the lady/man and found myself thinking, that's nice, yes I like that, Osborne sort your life out its time to leave the bar.

With the Italian exercise finished and behind us it was only a matter of weeks before we would be away again and this time it would be in Denmark. But still fresh in my mind was the thought of me lip locking this other man, and getting a handful of balls. For the next couple of weeks the lads had the up most pleasure of reminding me of this every day.

I had Transsexual mags appearing on my desk with telephone numbers highlighted on them. One of the lads even wore a dress, and had a wig on and was wearing makeup and walked past my office. As I looked up I thought who is that and then I noticed the army boots on his feet. Where are you going get in here, he minced his way to the door and with his hand on his hip he said in a very effeminate voice "I'm looking for the Sergeant Major can you help me". There was a huge roar of laughter along the corridor, and I realised everyone was in on it except me. The lads had even asked the OC if they could do this prank, and of course he had agreed.

But like everything else after a couple of weeks it had worn off, I took it all in good spirits and laughed about it with the boys. I could have done the opposite and not seen the funny side of their pranks and been a bastard. But I didn't I went down the route of I had fucked up, so let the lads have a laugh within reason at my expense, it was not hurting anyone and it certainly was not hurting me. I had already got there respect, but with the way that I dealt with this matter I had sealed that respect for good.

CHAPTER FORTY

The move out to Denmark went off without a hitch as did the main part of the exercise. After the exercise had finished we all had a couple of days to chill out and take in the sights. A couple of us were sat in this cafe come bar and were enjoying a couple of beers when this man mountain walked in, and sat down at a table and ordered.

A quick glance over to him followed by a smile broke the ice; he started talking to us in a very loud voice and gesturing for us to join him. We politely declined the offer and stayed where we were. His order eventually turned up and we could not take our eyes of off his meal. He had salad and potatoes in one bowl and in the other bowl there were a number of small fish about 2 inches in size and they were alive and swimming around.

We watched him take a fish by the tail and after banging the fishes head on the side of his plate, he just popped it into his mouth then in went some salad and potatoes, then he chewed it up and finally swallowed. After watching him repeat the eating process that was my signal to join his table. He seemed very happy and with bits of food stuck around his mouth, he delivered a heavy slap onto the middle of my back. This was followed by a big hello in his language and the plate of live fish was pushed in front of me.

He was grinning away and pointing to the fish with his big fat fingers and he obviously wanted me to try one. So with the loud support that I was now getting from the guys I went for it. I picked up a fish and banged its head on the plate and put it into my mouth. The fish was only half dead or it was its nerves but it was still wriggling around inside my mouth, so in went some salad and some potato and I crunched away.

The fish seemed to explode when you first chewed on it and the taste was rotten, so you mixed it as quickly as possible with the rest of the contents in your mouth and swallowed it. The stranger was laughing out loud which drew the attention of some of the locals and motioned for me to have another one. So as not to upset him or the little crowd that had now gathered around the table, I repeated the act once more. With the fish swallowed I pushed the bowl back to the man and was saying Yummy mmm, I'm full and of course thank you. I got lots of well dones from the locals and you're fucking mad from my guys but at least I had done it.

After a minute or two a very large beer and I mean large beer appeared in front of me the stranger had brought me it, and was sat there with his glass raised, so over I went and knocked glasses cheers my friend and took a mouthful.

I do not remember the time I actually left the cafe come bar to be honest I don't really remember leaving it. I never found out this strangers name, and

I never understood a word he had said to me. We communicated with each other by using the trusty sign language we got by and the best part is too strangers had had a brilliant day together.

We were now back in the UK and the deployment to Norway was only a few weeks away. There was a week's training organised for everyone for those who had been to Norway before this was a refresher week, to those who had never done or been involved in Artic Warfare this week was crucial. Having to learn how to operate the equipment that we would be using was not easy. There was a lot to take in but it was interesting and I was looking forward to getting out there, and putting what I had learnt in that week into practice.

With my head full of Norway, Christmas had come and passed me by without really noticing it. I had been to a number of functions over the Christmas period as it was par for the course for SSMs to attend. I am not complaining far from it but being out every night partying takes its toll on you. So when Christmas does eventually arrive you are pretty much fed up with it all. A couple of days after the festive season we were sat once again at the airport waiting to be taken to Norway.

CHAPTER FORTY-ONE

Touch down and here I am in the city of Bergan Norway and it's a bit nippy but not too bad. With all our kit collected from the airport we then boarded a couple of high class civilian coaches, lots of leg room and large comfy seats I could get used to traveling like this. We arrived at our hotel that's right our hotel and this was to be our base camp for the next couple of months. I could not believe it here I am on exercise and my bed is in a hotel. My room was on the ground floor and had a set of sliding doors that went out onto a balcony overlooking a lake. The hotel was built on the edge of this large lake and the water was crystal clear and pretty cold I might add. There was an indoor swimming pool and of course a sauna.
Basically the Military would take over a number of hotels in the Bergan/Voss area during the months of January to March so the British Army could carry out their Winter Warfare training. Along with the Royal Marines our unit had to undertake this type of training each year. This must of cost the MOD a small fortune, but who was I to complain I pay my taxes.
After a couple of days we had collected all our vehicles that we would need for the exercise and were parked up in the hotel car park. There were (BV 206s) and land rovers in the hotel car park, and now this nice hotel was looking more and more like an Army camp. with our bergan's laying in piles, and the crampons, skis and poles leant up against the wall. Every morning we would be out on the road running around this huge lake puffing and panting and trying to get used to breathing in the cold air (acclimatizing I think it's called). In the afternoon we were up in the mountains practicing our skiing skills.
I had never skied in my life and trying to get used to having these large planks strapped onto your feet, made life very hard. Trying to stand without falling over was a challenge but I soon mastered that trick. I would move forward about 3mtrs and down I would go face first in the snow. Up I would get and try again but back down into the snow I would go, again, and again, and again but I would not give up.
I got the name of Sniper because I was always in a snipers position face down. Every time I went over the lads would shout out snipers down and they all would have a good laugh.
After a day or two I could actually stay on my feet for about 50mtrs before I would crash but I was getting there. Digging snow holes, survival holes, and snow graves, was great fun and quite easy compared to digging trenches in the woods.

After a week I actually knew what I was meant to be doing and I could ski, not great but point me in the right direction and I would be on my way. When it came to turning well that was another problem, and I had to master it quickly especially when you have a bergan on your back. As soon as I would try to go left or right the weight of my bergan would tip me over, and yes I would hear snipers down.

The lake had now frozen over and the snow was falling almost every day, and I had a picture postcard view from my room.

There was one more objective left that we had to cover and that was the ice breaking drills. Basically the Instructors would go onto the ice with a chain saw and cut a large oblong hole into the ice. You would then line up one behind each other and with a rope tied around your waist and with one of the instructors holding the other end of the rope you would ski into the hole. You are in full kit and you have a bergan on your back. Once you are in the water you need to remove the bergan from your back get it onto your shoulder, and then onto the ice. Once that is done you have to swim to the other end of the hole which is about 4mtrs away, and then with the spiked end of each ski pole you have to stick them into the ice and drag yourself out if you can.

There was a small tent about 20 metres away from the hole and it had a big heater blowing hot air into the tent. That was where you went to warm up if you survived the freezing water. With the rope firmly fixed around my waist I got the call to start skiing into the hole. My heart was banging away so loud I'm sure I could hear it, and my brain was saying, no, this is not right what are you doing stop ,stop now.!

But I did not stop and I plunged straight into the freezing water and did not feel anything, nor did I hear anyone, had I died. This feeling lasted for about half a second and then it hit you. The freezing water goes straight through your clothes and was now trying to freeze your skin. My head felt like it was in some sort of vice and it was squeezing so hard it was trying to get my ears to meet in the middle. My heart was trying to detach itself from its arteries and valves, but thankfully it was still beating.

I got the pack of off my back and onto the ice and then floundered my way to the end of the hole. With my fingers frozen I managed to dig the ski poles into the ice and drag my sorry arse out of the water. With the help of others I managed to get out of my wet clothes and started to roll in the snow. This mad act does works believe me, even though it is a little strange to be naked rolling around in the snow. I then got myself into the tent and started to thaw out. I wanted to get back outside as soon as possible just so I could watch the lads do their ice breaking drills.

With the final briefing done and dusted it was a case of getting your arse into whatever BV 206 you had been assigned to travel in as we were moving out of the hotel for two weeks and into the mountains.

A BV 206 is a tracked vehicle which can move across the snow and ice without a problem. It comprises of two units the front unit is for the driver and about five passengers, then there is a separate unit attached to the rear this can hold more passengers and equipment if need be.

I was in the front vehicle along with four others and was sat directly behind the driver. The rain had started to fall and I was thinking to myself, typical just fucking typical.

After about twenty minutes driving we started to approach a tunnel and this tunnel runs straight through a mountain area and is about eight kilometre's long. There was an articulated vehicle exiting the tunnel and we all noticed that it was starting to weave across the road. Our driver slowed down and took evasive action and drove off the road and onto the verge. We could not get over any further because we had the side of a mountain in the way. The truck that had exited the tunnel had now jacked knifed and was heading straight towards us and it was not slowing down and the reason why, because he was now aquaplaning.

There was an almighty bang and that was all I remember about the impact. When I came round there was a lot of blood everywhere and my driver was screaming my leg my leg. I was covered in blood but I was not sure if it was mine or somebody else's, but there was loads of it and it was on me. I gathered my senses and thought right Sergeant Major get out and see what damage is done and to get things organised. There was a massive hole on the side of the vehicle and I went to climb through it, but all I done was fall onto the road. As I lay there I could not believe the carnage in the road the rear unit of the BV 206 had totally disintegrated there was just nothing left.

One of the lads ran over to me and put a field dressing onto my head, I was awake and knew what was going on around me but I was helpless to do anything except just sit there.

I knew I was pretty smashed up because my left leg was at an unusual angle compared to my right leg. My left shoulder was not where it should be it was just hanging down my side. And when they applied two more field dressings to my head I knew there was a big problem. Each field dressing can hold up to one pint of blood, I was now on my third one. It took the rescue and ambulance teams about thirty minutes to get to us, but the lads had done a fantastic job in dealing with the situation. Myself and the driver where put into an ambulance and away we went heading for the main hospital in Bergan.

I kept going in and out of consciousness as we made our way to the hospital or so I thought, and there were people running around everywhere when we arrived. Drips put into my arms, people looking into my eyes, they were asking do I know who I am, where are you, and can you see me, and so on. I had broken my left Femur, my left shoulder had punctured the shoulder socket, and my left collar bone was broken. I had a massive cut on the left hand side of my head and there was this nurse talking to me as she was stitching me up. Having been pumped with pain killers I was talking to the nurse about what had happened and of course how many stiches she was putting into my head. We stopped on eighty nine and this was not because she had finished, it was because a senior policeman had come into the room and asked if I was Sergeant Major Osborne. He then informed me that three of my soldiers had been killed in the accident and told me there names.

After getting my head and broken bits sorted out, I was put into a room with the three others guys that had been hurt in the accident one of which was my driver. He had a mangled foot and badly broken leg but he would survive. A Norwegian woman came into the room and said she was a counselor and if we needed to talk about it then she was there for us. We politely told her to go fourth and multiply and we would get through this in our own way.

Word of the accident had got back to the UK in fact it was on Sky News and like everything else when there is a tragic incident like this then those back at camp have got to get the correct information ASAP and then inform the families of those involved straight away.

I said I was in and out of consciousness in the back of the ambulance well in fact I had died twice as we made our way to the hospital. This information had got back to UK and the word on the street was that I was dead. When my wife (at the time) answered the door she must have gone into shock, because the Padre was standing there along with a female officer. They told her about the accident in Norway and that I had been killed. After a while the Padre left but the female officer stayed with my wife and two children. An hour or so later he was back saying, Mrs Osborne your husband is alive he had died in fact he had died twice but he is alive now and is in hospital in Bergan.

The emotions that women must of gone through in that one hour must have been terrible, but they were nothing compared to what the parents of the three young lads must have been going through. After a couple of days I was allowed to leave the hospital and could not wait to get back to the hotel and see the Boss and the lads. The exercise had been put on hold for a few days so at least I would see them all before they went out the next day. That evening everyone was in the bar and the OC took this moment to say a few words about the three guys who had died and also praised the way the other lads kept themselves together at the scene of the accident. After the Boss had finished speaking we all raised our glasses in memory of the three lads.

CHAPTER FORTY-TWO

The atmosphere within the Sqn was still very subdued some of the lads could not get there head around the fact that we had lost three very good lads, so quickly and in such tragic circumstances. On returning back to our camp in the UK everyone went on leave for a couple of weeks. A couple of weeks away from the green machine, and away from the military environment does wonders for the mind and body.
Over the next four months it was basically working within the camp. This quite period always had two sides to it one side was good the other side was bad. A lot of the lads could get away on courses that they needed to do so they could be in the running for promotion. Outdoor courses such as rock climbing, abseiling, and canoeing were also high on the list so people got away on these adventure training courses.
If you're in camp you get picked for everything ranging from guard duties, work parties for this and that, getting involved in parades and to cap it all the RSM sees what you are doing every day, and gets involved even though it has nothing to do with him and will become a pain in the arse. The reason he will do this is because he is bored out of his mind and misses not being involved with the men.
The RSM answers to one man and one man only and that is the Commanding Officer. Now the RSM overseas the SSMs of each squadron making sure that discipline is being carried out correctly. Well if the SSM is doing his job correctly and everything is working just fine then the RSM is sat in his office looking for a problem.
He will always find a problem if one of the lads turns up in shit order for guard one day, then that is the perfect excuse for him to visit the sqn and that is all he needs. He will then find fault in everything within the Sqn. The Sqn is in shit state Sergeant Major and the guys are in rag order, the outside areas are filthy, and the whole sqn needs a fucking haircut, what have you been doing Sergeant Major get yourself and the Sqn sorted out.
He will then go back to his office feeling very proud of himself and will gladly say to the CO "Sir I have just given so and so Sqn a bollocking and told the SSM to get a grip of his Sqn as they were a bag of shit, so I gave them a good kick up the arse". This is all part of the game you will not do anything different, and the next time he sees you it will be, well done SSM I see you got those problems sorted out, Yes Sir I did Sir.
It was time to get out of the camp again and yes we were on our way back to Denmark for a couple of weeks, but the difference being that this time everyone's deploying. The CO and his staff and if the CO is coming then that means the RSM is coming. You just have to pray that your location is

miles away from the Head Quarters, because the last thing you want is waking up to that lot every morning. We got our wish and were about eight kilometres away from the funny farm.

The exercise went well and to be honest the RSM was not that bad he would pop over for a chat now and then with the lads, and sometimes stay in our location for a couple of hours. He would say to me, I had to get away from those muppets, sitting there and listening to them day in day out is sending me mad. So I have told the boss that I think it would be a good idea to visit the Sqns daily and see if they are ok and get any feedback.

We got a visit one morning from the CO but we knew he was coming the RSM had tipped me off so everything and everyone was ready for him I offered to show the RSM around the camp while the OC entertained the Colonel. Denmark was another success for everyone if the CO gets lots of well dones and pats on the back, then us mere mortals get an easy time and of course a well done.

With the Sqn back of a week's leave there was just one last task to do before the end of the year and that was to organise an Open Day for a number of the Senior Military Officers from the MOD a few Brigadiers and the odd General. The theme would be Norway and the winter warfare training that we carry out each year. We would also be showing them the equipment that we use while carrying out this training.

The day arrived and while all the visitors were down the officers mess having tea and scones we were putting the final touches to our displays and they were looking good. The lads had done a brilliant job in setting it all up, and all of those taking part in the demonstrations were on the ball.

The officers went from stand to stand and were very impress with what they saw and also what they heard from some of the men. The officers asked many questions and the soldiers gave them honest answers. One question asked by an officer was about the Polk (sledge) that we pulled around. He wanted to know if it was easy to pull and was it very manoeuvrable. The soldier answered no sir it's a pain in the fucking arse, it's too heavy and out of date we need lighter ones. Instead of the officer walking away, he started asking how do you mean he was actually interested in the soldiers answer, I just moved on and left them talking.

The last demonstration of the day was taking place in one of the classrooms where my Senior Artic Warfare Instructor was going to give a lecture on the clothing that we wear during our time in Norway. He was a Scotsman, about 5ft 9in stocky and held the rank of Sgt, and was by far the best person to give this lecture.

The room was packed with all the visitors plus the CO and of course the RSM. I thanked them all for coming and hoped that they had enjoyed themselves and hopefully would leave here more the wiser in what we do and how we achieve it while in Norway. I then handed them over to my

senior instructor and stood to the side of the clothing display.
He was very good answering questions in great detail and explaining some of the problems that some bits of clothing give us. He pushed the point that once our clothing was wet it would stay wet for days, whereas similar clothing worn by civilians would dry in a matter of hours, good lad he was pushing for better clothing. He then picked up the large hat that we all wear out there it has pull down flaps that cover your ears and it has puffed up lining inside that keeps your head warm.

He put it on his head with the side flaps down and said Gentleman this is called a DILAC hat and it is worn like this. I turned and looked at him and thought don't go down that line and prayed nobody would ask the obvious but they did. Someone said "Sergeant what does dilac stand?" for, I could have collapsed No, don't answer him but it was too late. He stood there with this hat on his head with the ear muffs down, and his chest sticking out and said in a very proud Scottish accent Sir It stands for "Don't I look a C---". The officer just stared at him in disbelief and said (oh I see). There were a couple of sniggers around the room but no more comments or questions with regards to the Dilac hat.

The Christmas functions were nearly upon us yet again and we all knew what that meant NORWAY was not that far away. So it was back into refresher training for most of us, and of course a big learning curve for those who had joined us during the year. The month of December is a social month for all of us it is just function after function, and being a SSM you get invited to lots of Regimental functions, Sqn parties, Troop functions, so it takes its toll on you again. But you have to attend these Sqn functions because these are the guys you have worked with and bollocked during the year, and now it's time to sit down with them and have a couple of wet ones.

CHAPTER FORTY-THREE

It was good to get back to Norway and the snow had already fallen in Bergan making it a very picturesque city. The drive to the hotel would also take us past the very point of where the accident had happened last year. The hotel had not changed a bit and they still had the same staff. Who would have thought we had been away for nine months I had the same room and the view had not changed a bit, in fact it looked better than before.

On the anniversary of the accident myself and about twenty sqn personnel went and paid our respects to the three lads who had died in the horrific accident one year to the day. A plaque was drilled into the rock face (which is still there today) and a small service was held. For those of you who are wondering what happened to the driver of the truck, well he broke both his legs and was in shock, oh yes, and he was also drunk when he hit our BV206, no sympathy.

With the memorial service over it was back to the training and the preparation for the deployment into the mountains was moving at 100 miles an hour. The day arrived and as we mounted up into our BV206s you just could not help thinking that this was day ja vu. All you can do is block out any thoughts about what had happened last year and concentrate on the job in hand. There were six of us traveling in the front vehicle and four out of the six had also been in the front vehicle last year. We were approaching the tunnel again but this time there was no truck and it was dry. As we safely passed the spot that had devastated so many lives last year, the four of us let out a big YES get in there. That was the release of a lot of tension and adrenalin that had built up over the last couple of days and if there were any ghosts to bury then we had buried them.

The exercise went well lots of snow and living in snow holes, and of course freezing your nuts off at night. They say that if the temperature drops below -30 then the exercise would get cancelled. It never went below that mark even with me covering the thermometer with blocks of ice.

But we all survived and everyone got back to the hotel in one piece. After all the equipment was cleaned and handed back in one piece it was time to sit back and relax for a couple of days. Transport was laid on for those who wanted to go down to the town during the day. People could go out onto the frozen lake with the locals who would then drill a hole into the ice and then sit on their little stalls and fish.

How boring you think not at all, you see the norgies enjoy a drink and so they drive their car or jeep onto the ice and park it up. In the back would be a cool box packed with beer and then to my amazement they brought out a BBQ built on a stand and fired it up. With great food and beer going down to easy you forgot just how cold it was standing on a frozen lake supposedly fishing.

With the adventures of Norway behind us and a couple of weeks leave it was back to the normal life of being in camp and under the watchful eyes of the RSM here we go again. The next exercise which was to be my last with the Sqn was going to take place in Turkey during the month of September and October.

It was very hot when we arrived on the advance party and like Italy we were to be housed in a huge tented camp the only difference being was that, there was a Turkish soldier every ten metres and this was repeated all the way around the perimeter of the camp. How strange I thought but it was not until night time that I understood why they were there.

One of the Turkish soldiers would blow a whistle then the one next to him would blow his whistle and this went on from soldier to soldier and carried on around the camp. Blowing these whistles had two functions the first being that the sound of the whistle would keep the packs of dogs out of the camp, and secondly you knew the person next to you was still there and importantly they were alive.

With that taken on board and the fact that the main party had arrived it was time to get ready for the deployment. Every exercise is different from the locations, to different people, different objectives, and of course different countries and each country has different insects to worry about. I was digging a shell scrape with my combat jacket on, when I felt a stinging sensation in the middle of my back. This lad hit me on the back and then said don't move sir a little bit late I thought but I thanked him. I took my Combat Jacket off and there was this bug the size of a large moth with a drill attached to the front of his head. He had stuck his drill through the material of my jacket and into my back, and now I had a painful lump the size of an egg in the centre of my back. The ants in our area where massive and were at least 1 inch long and there were thousands of them. If you stamped on a couple and killed them watch out because a message would get out to the rest of the ants and before you knew it there was thousands heading your way.

The Turkish Army is a bit like the Italian Army it is made up of conscripts and these lads do not get paid much if they get paid anything at all. I had the same problem as with the Italians, I would turn up in their location and if they were there it would be a bonus and if they were sober well that would have meant we would have had to have had a public holiday. It was so frustrating for me as well as everyone else but what can you do. Finally the exercise came to an end and I think everybody was happy about that.

So as always there was a couple of free days to be had and after we had cleaned up and got all the equipment handed back it was chill out time. Health and hygiene is a big thing within the Army and we all do as much as we can to keep on top of it. There are some countries that we exercise in that don't take it as serious as us and Turkey was just one of those countries.

A few of us had popped down town and had chosen this little bar to go into and have a couple of drinks. It was a little dark but looked good enough for us squaddies to go and have a drink in. There was a bench seat that was fitted to the wall and went around three quarters of the bar. After sitting there for a couple of minutes we noticed that we had thousands of ants walking over our laps. They would walk over me then over one of the lads and so on, until they got to where they were going. We had obviously sat down on their walk way so not to be out done they decided just to walk over the top of us. We finished our beers and left the bar leaving the ants to carry on with whatever they were doing.

Later on that evening we were getting hungry so we found a kebab shop. We all ordered a kebab each and then watched in amazement as to what happened next. The meat was not turning around on its little spit and the heaters were not lit but the meat looked cooked. The guy behind the counter had long greasy hair, unshaven and was wearing the dirtiest chef's whites I had ever seen. He walked over to the meat and flicked a towel in that direction and that disturbed about fifty flies that were having their lunch.

As he put down his cigarette on the edge of the counter, he started to cough and so he put his hands up to his mouth and coughed into them. Then he lit the heaters and with his bare hands (remember he had just coughed into them) placed them onto the meat and started to turn the meat around on the spit. Once the spit had taken over and was turning the meat, he just wiped his hands onto his jacket and started to cut up the pita bread.

Even after watching this show of Health and Hygiene at its best we all waited for our kebabs to be made up, we then paid for them and said thank you very much.

While we were munching our way through these kebabs we all agreed to meet in the toilets the next day. Believe it or not nobody was there not one of us was ill how amazing was that, or was it just luck.

My time in the sqn was coming to an end I had been selected for promotion to the rank of Warrant Officer Class 1 (RSM) and was due to take up the position of RSM in March 94. So there was no Norway for me that year but that did not worry me too much, as I had a lot to get done before my posting date. The boys went to Norway and I remained back at camp doing this and that and then finally moving to my new post.

CHAPTER FORTY-FOUR

It was September 1976 when I first walked into the camp of Buller Barracks and started my basic training. This was the place that I got bollocked continuously and was put behind the guard so many times I lost count. I was told on a number of occasions to get out of the army because you are a waster Osborne and the army don't have wasters. But I will always remember one thing and this is the only bit of advice I think I ever took on board. My intake CPL took me to one side just after I had received another bollocking and said (Remember whatever they say or do they cannot make you pregnant).

I must have done something right because seventeen years later I was walking back into that same camp, not as a new recruit who thought he knew everything, but as the Regimental Sergeant Major who knew a lot about everything. I was so proud of myself to think I had gone full circle. I had seen many places and had served in a few hostile countries but now I am back to where I started my army career Aldershot.

I will always remember my first day as RSM of the regt, it is something that will stay with me forever, all the other days do not really count. It's a bit like fishing the first fish you ever catch as a lad is the best feeling in the world, when you catch another one of course it's good, but you don't get the same feeling as the first one you caught.

After the compulsory Monday morning regimental parade I dismissed the officers and my SSMs and spoke to the men. These are the guys who drive the big green machine twenty four hours a day, every day, every week, every month, year in year out. The SNCOs and Officers outline what needs to be done and give guidance, but it's those on the ground that get the jobs done. If you fail to get these people on your side and fail to get them working for you then you are knackered.

I introduced myself and explained to them all that I have an open door policy and if after you have gone through the correct chain of command, and you're still not happy about something you can come and see me. But remember I will always back my Warrant Officers and SNCOs so don't waste my time over silly petty things.

I am a modern type of RSM, if I speak to you about something then speak back and tell me what you are doing and why. If you see me down town which you will and you want to speak to me, do not address me as Sir, or stand up if I walk into a pub. Just call me by my name Steve or Ossie and just chat to me as normal. I won't insult your intelligence but when at work then it's different.

That was the most important thing to get done on my first day informing the men what you are like and what you expect from them, it puts them at ease. Speaking to your Warrant Officers and SNCOs that can come later on over the next few days. My past had preceded me so before I had even took up post everybody knew what I was like.

During my interview with my commanding officer he made a comment about my haircut, he thought it was rather offensive looking. I did not agree and told him that a grade one all over was a smart military and hygienic haircut. I then said to him that I found it strange that in today's modern world, you do not have a television and only hire one out for a couple of weeks when your daughter comes home from boarding school. So we clashed a bit on our first meeting but so be it I had not got to this position by being a yes man.

Days turned to weeks and being the RSM was just like any other rank you had your job to do which you done, but you also had to watch over all the other jobs that needed doing within the regt. I was starting to understand why my previous RSMs would come down to the Sqns for a chat or a moan. It was now so obvious they missed getting involved with the daily running of a Sqn.

The RSM would not get involved with the daily working parades or the day to day management of the men. The RSM was up in the Ivory towers cut off from all this and after seventeen years of always being involved some way or another it was strange to be that isolated. Of course being the big cheese has its good points and great perks.

Nobody dares to ask you what you are doing or where you are going. I would get my work done then say to the Colonel, Sir "I am popping up to the Sergeants mess as there is a bit of mess business to get done so if you need me sir, that is where I will be".

Being the President of the Sgts Mess is another task you have to take on one which I revelled in. Summer Balls, Christmas functions where always a lavish affair, and I never penny pinched on either one. Regimental dinners were also a very pompous occasion, with lots of wine and port getting consumed. Being the President of the mess gave me the chance to call on a few people that I had known in my past and they were the RCT Band.

They would come along and entertain the mess with some great music. And the Corps of Drums were second to none they were brilliant and everyone loved them. Normally when the Corps band had finished playing then they would pack up and leave.

No chance of that I had served in the Gulf with these lads and they had done me proud. Now it was my time to show my appreciation, so all there drinks would get put onto my drinks bill, and this would always be over the hundred pound mark. This bill would be put against drinks for the mess guests and would be written off, just one of the perks.

I would go down town on a Saturday and put my bets on the football and horses, and then I would go to the pub for a beer or two. The pubs I would go to were the ones that I used when I was here twelve years ago and they had not changed a bit.

I would see some of the lads in the pubs and we would sit down and talk about footie or whatever, it was great for them and of course it was brilliant for me, this is what I was missing.

Some sniveling shit bag had told the CO that I was going down town on a Saturday and having a beer with the lads. The CO actually asked me why I would do this, and what was wrong with drinking in the mess. There's nothing wrong with drinking in the mess Sir, it's just that they can be boring bastards up there, and as for drinking down town Sir, I do not see that being a problem. Somebody once told me "Never forget where you came from we all started at the bottom, and I was once a Private soldier Sir, and I would have loved it if my SSM or RSM had been more approachable back then". We never always saw eye to eye me and the boss but I was never going to change the way that I done things.

The life of the RSM is a strange one, you are the most powerful man in the Regt after the CO but then you don't have anyone to be in command of as each Sqn has its own SSM. You do not have the daily hands on with the men of the sqns, and I personally found that very hard to except.

I had made it to the top of the tree and to be honest I was not really happy. From day one in the army I had always wanted to work my way up the ranks. And now I had reached the top of the tree I must admit it's not all it's made out to be. There was always hundred and sixty eight WO1s at any one time in the British Army, and of course I was extremely proud and honored to have been one of those hundred and sixty eight. Not everyone gets to be a RSM and of course not everyone wants that responsibility, but I did and I had got there by hard work and of course a bit of luck on the way. The normal route for the RSM to go after he had finished his appointment was to apply for a short term commission, and this would be for a maximum of five years. I was told a couple of times from those high up that it was expected of me to take this commission and to do a further five years as a Captain.

What would I be doing as a Captain well I will tell you? I would be sat behind a desk pushing bits of paper about, listening to different soldier's welfare problems like my wife has left me, I don't have any money to cover my debts.

No thank you that was not for me, I am sorry but I will stay as a WO1 for the next couple of years as I am not interested in getting commissioned. Well this did not go down too well in manning and records and they told me so. Do you realise we have spent a lot of time and money and effort on you Mr. Osborne, grooming you for the RSMs position and then the natural transition to an officer.

I am not a person easily shocked but that attitude pissed me off so my answer to them was, "I have given you nineteen years of my life busting my balls off in the Falklands, five years total in Northern Ireland, the 1st Gulf War and that's just to name a few things I have done for the British Army, I have seen people dying, I have seen many people dead and I have lost some good friends along the way, so I have also put a lot of time and effort into my career and I am not interested in becoming an Officer".

The last two and a half years of my Military career was holding the appointment of TCWO (Transport Control Warrant Officer) and I was back to being happy again. I had a fleet of two hundred vehicles and a staffing of hundred civilians, and about fifty military personnel. Our role was to supply all types of military transport for the whole of the Aldershot area. I had the fuel budget, servicing budget, and of course the civilian overtime budget to manage on a daily basis.

I was back amongst people and being involved in the planning of all the daily details was very satisfying even when the odd one went wrong. Getting up and going to work in the mornings was again fun and I looked forward to it every day I was there.

My old office was across the road from where I was now working, and I would see the RSM walking about waving his stick and shouting at people because he had to, it was part of the job.

Many people have said to me, Steve it must have been great being the RSM and they are taken back when I say not really in fact it was the worst position that I held during my time in the army.

Then the day finally came and I was to leave the British Army in fact it was quite simple really, all the paper work had already been completed i.e. my medical, the pension, all things like that have to be done prior to me leaving. I walked into the Admin office and handed over my Identity card to the chief clerk, and in return he gave me a stack of papers and booklets giving you information about how to adjust too living in Civi Street. I then made my way towards the guard room and the entrance to the camp. As I approached the barriers the lad on the gate lifted one of the barriers up for me and came to attention.

He was only a young lad and as I passed him I thought good luck son have a great career because I have had a fantastic one. My last words I ever said while serving in the Green Machine was to this young lad carrying out gate guard, I turned to him and said "REMEMBER WHAT EVER THEY SAY OR DO THEY CANNOT MAKE YOU PREGNANT", and he laughed and said "cheers for that Sir"

I really hope you have enjoyed reading my book as much as I enjoyed writing it. I have been retired from the British Army for the past 13 years now. After having a bar in Portugal for nine of those years I decided to sell up and travel. You can follow me on my travels through my Blog. Contact details below.

https://stevenosborne53.wordpress.com
https://www.steveosbornebritisharmy.com
mailto:stevenosborne53ya@yahoo.com

Printed in Great Britain
by Amazon